Math + Sci
A Solution

Authors

John Campopiano

Judith Hillen

John Kinnear

Walt Laidlaw

Nancy Rice

Karen Zahlis

Illustrator

Sheryl Mercier

Editors

Larry Ecklund   Arthur Wiebe

AIMS Education Foundation • Fresno, California

AIMS (**A**ctivities **I**ntegrating **M**athematics and **S**cience) began in 1981 with a grant from the National Science Foundation. The non-profit AIMS Education Foundation publishes hands-on instructional materials (books and the monthly AIMS Newsletter) that integrate curricular disciplines such as mathematics, science, language arts, and social studies. The Foundation sponsors a national program of professional development through which educators may gain both an understanding of the AIMS philosophy and expertise in teaching by integrated, hands-on methods.

ISBN 1-881431-06-1

Printed in the United States of America

Table of Contents

Skills Chart iv

Chinese Proverb v

Introduction 1

It's A Shoe In! 2

Unique U 4

On Your Own Two Feet 7

    Creature Features 14

Super Sleuth 16

Mini Metric Olympics 19

    Mini Metric Olympics II 30

    Metric Scavenger Hunt 31

Cool It! 32

Hot Stuff 34

Corny Comparisons 37

Weight Watchers 39

Second Guessing 42

Chaotic Computing 44

It's Simply Marble-ous 51

Count and Crunch — "m & m's"® candies 55

What's in the Bag— "m & m's"® candies 58

Dealing with Data 61

Practically Pi 65

Just Drop It 68

Screen Test 71

Trial and Error Learning 74

Graph-Feet-EE 79

The Penny Sort & Nickel Dates 83

Rubber Band Stretch 96

Rubber Band Shoot 99

It's Bean Fun! 101

The Big Banana Peel 105

Going Bananas 107

Sample Grids 115

Index to Skills

MATH SKILLS

Attributes 1, 3
Applying Formulas 34, 36
Averaging 13, 17, 19, 21, 26, 28, 37, 39
Calculator Usage 13
Counting 22, 34, 36
Decimal Computation 13, 19, 24
Equations 13, 14, 24, 26, 34, 36, 39
Estimating 9, 13, 14, 21, 22, 28, 30
Formula Usage 13, 14, 26, 34, 36, 39
Fractions 19
Frequency Tables 19, 33
Graphing 3, 10, 11, 17, 19, 21, 24, 26, 29, 30, 33, 34, 36, 39
Logic 2, 3, 5, 7, 37
Measuring Area 9
Measuring Length 9, 17, 24, 28, 30, 34, 36
Measuring Mass 9, 13, 34, 36, 39
Measuring Temperature 10, 11
Measuring Volume 9, 12
Patterns 34, 36
Percent 3, 13, 14, 19, 33, 39
Permutations 33
Predicting 9, 12, 13, 21
Probability 33, 37
Problem Solving 2, 5, 37
Ratios 12, 13, 14, 22, 37, 39
Rounding Decimals 19, 24
Sampling 22, 33, 37
Set Theory 1
Sorting 2, 5
Tabulating 21, 33
Timing 15, 29
Using Tables 5, 28
Venn Diagrams 1
Whole Number Computation 15, 17, 21

SCIENCE PROCESSES

Generalizing 10, 12, 26, 28, 34, 36, 37, 39
Hypothesizing 21, 33
Inferring 21, 33
Interpreting Data 10, 11, 17, 19, 21, 22, 24, 26, 28, 29, 30, 36, 39
Observing 1, 2, 3, 5, 7, 10, 11, 13, 19, 22, 28
Recording Data . . . . All investigations
Variables 24, 26, 34, 36

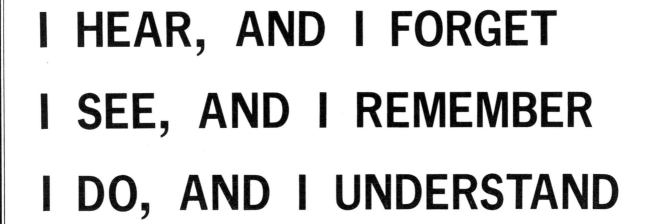

I HEAR, AND I FORGET

I SEE, AND I REMEMBER

I DO, AND I UNDERSTAND

–Chinese Proverb

Introduction

This book may be described as a sample of innovative activities that correlate to mathematics and science in a unique and exciting way. These highly motivting investigations invite students and teachers to explore, discover, and enjoy the many fascinating elements of our world. The investigations employ a wide variety of readily available and easily understood materials—from marbles to "m & m"® candies to old shoes and rubber balls.

The twenty-five investigations presented here are sequenced from simple to complex according to these science processes:

A.   Observing and Classifying

B.   Measuring

D.   Estimating, Predicting, and Hypothesizing

D.   Controlling Variables

E.   Gathering and Recording Data

F.   Interpreting Data

G.   Applying and Generalizing

While the experiences are ordered in this manner, be encouraged to select any of the activities to supplement your own curriculum

It is the sincere desire of the writing team that these curricular materials will encourage and challenge teachers and students in the endeavor to integrate math and science.

IT'S A SHOE-IN!

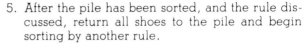

I. Topic Area
Observation and classification.

II. Introductory Statement
In this activity, students will use their own shoes and those of their classmates to develop observational skills. Shoe characteristics will be sketched or listed on the student sheet. A guessing game format is used to make the activity even more appealing.

III.

Math Skills	Science Processes
a. Attributes	a. Observing
b. Set Theory	b. Classifying
c. Venn Diagrams (optional)	c. Recording Data

IV. Materials (per class)
A large pile of 20 or more student shoes

V. Key Question
"Can you guess the characteristic being used to sort the shoes?"

VI. Background Information
Attributes or characteristics that may be used include: shoe color, shoe type, shoe lace color, type of sole, etc.

VII. Management Suggestions
1. Have students stand or sit in a semi-circle around the pile of shoes.
2. Students should put both of their shoes in the pile.
3. The estimated time required for this investigation is one class period of 45-60 minutes.

VIII. Procedure
1. A pile of as many different shoes as possible is collected from the students and placed on the floor.
2. The teacher announces that he/she will begin sorting the shoes into two piles by following some rule, based on one characteristic or attribute.
3. The students are to guess the rule by which the teacher is sorting.
4. Students who think they know the rule can finish sorting the pile using that rule, one student at a time, so that the teacher can make sure that his/her guess is correct.

5. After the pile has been sorted, and the rule discussed, return all shoes to the pile and begin sorting by another rule.
6. The teacher should initially sort the pile using one characteristic as the rule, such as: one pile of brown shoes and one pile of shoes that are not brown. After several such trials the teacher should try sorting the pile using two or more characteristics as the rule, such as: one pile of brown shoes with heels and one pile of all the other shoes.
7. After this activity has been repeated several times, students are to sketch and label five different shoe characteristics or attributes that were used in sorting, using boxes 2-6 on the "Shoe Sort" student worksheet. Or the student worksheet may be used to simply *list* the various attributes.

IX. What the Students Will Do
1. Guess or identify the characteristics being used to sort.
2. Sketch and label, or list five shoe characteristics used in this activity.

X. Discussion
1. What attribute do all the shoes have in common? (Worn on feet, all have soles, etc.)
2. How many attributes does a simple object such as a shoe have? (Many, several, etc.)
3. What are some attributes that most shoes have? (Answers might include laces, no heels, soles, etc.)
4. What are some attributes that few shoes have? (Answers might include purple color, heels, etc.)

XI. Extension
1. A complete list of their classmates' personal attributes could be compiled and graphed.
2. Venn diagrams could be constructed to show some of the observed characteristics.
3. By using pictures of animals, students could develop their own lists of animal attributes.
4. Students could make tree diagrams like the one shown below to sort and classify their shoes.

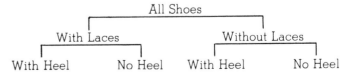

IT'S A SHOE-IN!

Shoe Sort

1.

2.

3.

4.

5.

6.

Unique U

I. Topic Area
Observation and classification.

II. Introductory Statement
The students are to sort themselves according to their attributes (sex, hair color, type of clothing, etc.) until each student is in a group by himself/herself. In searching for a solution, students will learn a great deal about attributes that make them the same and different from everyone else in the class.

III. Math Skills
a. Logical Thinking
b. Sorting
c. Problem Solving

Science Processes
a. Observing
b. Classifying
c. Recording Data

IV. Materials
Sorting tree on a transparency
Overhead projector and screen.

V. Key Question
"What attributes make you a unique and special person?"

VI. Background Information
The students will be looking for attributes relevant to particular members of a group. They will choose from among these attributes to discover a category into which to place themselves. They will use a tree diagram which has two branches at every separation point.

VII. Management Suggestions
1. Estimated time: one 45 minute class period.

VIII. Procedure
1. When students come to a consensus on an attribute, the teacher will record this attribute on the overhead transparency. This will be done for each decision.
2. Starting with the whole class, the students will decide how to divide themselves into two groups based on one attribute.
3. The groups will move to opposite sides of the room.
4. Each of these groups will divide itself into two groups based on one attribute which need not be the same for each group. These will separate themselves into four places in the classroom.

5. This process will continue until each person is by himself or herself.
6. As soon as any student is by himself or herself, that student returns to his or her seat and traces his or her own particular attributes on the sorting tree. See the sample copy for these examples: Mary Jane is a student, a girl with long hair, and she is tall; Bobby is a student, a boy with short hair, and he is short.
7. A typical procedure might be as follows:
   Teacher: "What is one way you can sort your-selves into two groups?"
   Students: "Boys and girls." (Students do so.)
   Teacher: "Can you divide each group again?"
   Students: "Long hair and short hair." (Students divide again.)
   Teacher: "How many groups are there now?"
   Students: "Four."

IX. What the Students Will Do
1. Students will sort themselves according to various attributes of their choosing.
2. Each student will trace his or her own attributes on a tree diagram.

X. Discussion
1. Which attributes are the most general? (Those on the left side of the tree diagram.)
2. Which attributes are the most specific? (Those on the right side of the tree diagram.)
3. Which attributes made you a special and unique person in this classroom? (Answers will vary.)

XI. Extension
1. Sort buttons using the following attributes: 2 hole or 4 hole; round or straight; big or little; brown or not brown; etc. Other attributes may be selected by students.
2. Sort leaves by having students collect leaves. Use attributes such as: needles or whole leaves; branched or unbranched leaves; rough or smooth edged leaves; fine or coarse veined leaves; heart shaped or arrowhead shaped leaves; etc.
3. Classify animals by listing different kinds of animals on the overhead and having students sort the animals according to physical attributes.

Unique U

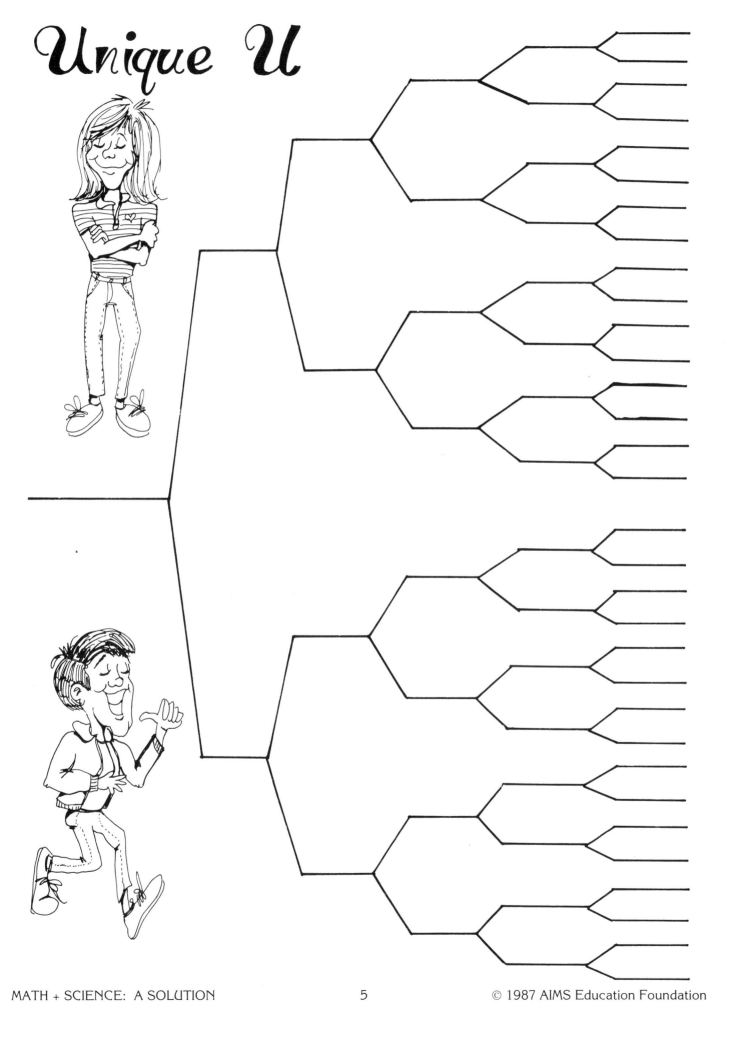

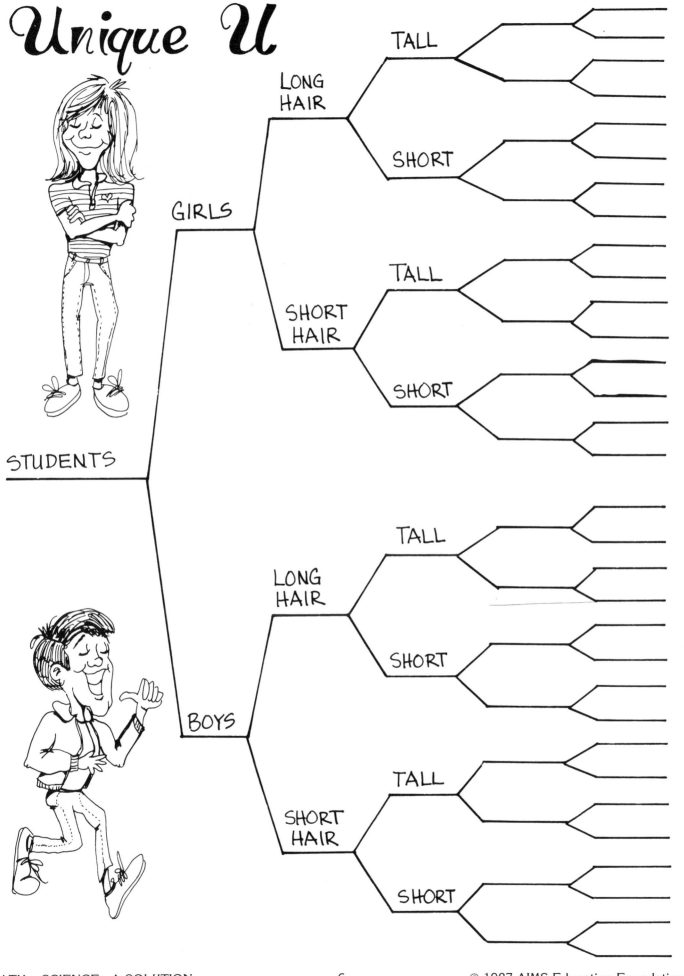

Unique U

GIRLS
- LONG HAIR
  - TALL
  - SHORT
- SHORT HAIR
  - TALL
  - SHORT

STUDENTS

BOYS
- LONG HAIR
  - TALL
  - SHORT
- SHORT HAIR
  - TALL
  - SHORT

On Your Own Two Feet

I. Topic Area
Observation and classification.

II. Introductory Statement
In this investigation, the students will observe and record the characteristics or attributes of their different shoes. By recording these characteristics on a data table, they will be able to identify a mystery shoe. A statistical analysis of these shoes will reveal the percentage of each type of shoe in the class, percentages of shoes with heels and laces, and a graphic representation of shoe sizes.

III. Math Skills
  a. Attributes
  b. Logical Thinking
  c. Computing Percent
  d. Graphing

Science Processes
  a. Observing
  b. Classifying
  c. Recording Data

IV. Materials
One shoe from each student.
Roll of masking tape.

V. Key Questions
1. Can you identify the mystery shoe based on its characteristics?
2. What percentage of your class is wearing tennis or running shoes?
3. What percentage of your class is wearing shoes with heels?
4. What percentage of your class is wearing shoes with laces?
5. What is the most common shoe size in your class?

VI. Background Information
1. To compute the percent of each type: divide the number of that type by the total number of shoes and multiply by 100.
2. Possible materials for soles might include leather, rubber, canvas, plastic, etc.

VII. Management Suggestions
1. Have all students place one of their shoes in a pile on the floor.
2. Using masking tape, number each shoe with a different number.
3. Estimated time to complete this investigation is one or two 45 minute class periods.

VIII. Procedure
Part I
1. Distribute one or more of Student Worksheet, page 9, depending on the total number of shoes in the pile.
2. Number each shoe with masking tape.
3. Start passing each shoe from student to student. Each student is to record the necessary information about each shoe in terms of the ten (10) characteristics shown at the top of the Student Worksheet.
4. When the students have recorded this information for all the shoes in the pile, the shoes are once again returned to the pile.
5. The teacher then picks up a shoe, removes the number (so that the students cannot see it), and begins describing some of its characteristics.
6. The first student to guess the correct shoe number gets to pick a shoe from the pile, remove the number, and describe the shoe's characteristics to the other students.

Part II
Use the information tabulated on Student Worksheet, page 9 to determine percentage of each shoe type, percent with heels, percent with laces, and the shoe size graph.

IX. What the Students Will Do
1. Complete a data table that will compare each of the shoes in a pile for ten different shoe attributes.
2. Identify the mystery shoe by comparing the characteristics recorded on their data table with those described by the teacher.
3. Determine the class percentage for shoe type, shoes with heels, and shoes with laces.
4. Make a bar graph showing class shoe sizes and number of each size.

X. Discussion
1. If two different shoe numbers have all ten attributes the same, must they be the same type of shoe, exactly? (No, but probably very similar)
2. Which of the ten attributes would be most important in terms of comfort? (Size, shoe type, materials of shoe, heel, laces, etc.)
3. What are some other shoe attributes that we could observe? (New or old, round or square toe, over or under the ankle, etc.)

4. How many separate ways could we group the shoes based on one characteristic? (At least 10, probably more)

5. What are some other groups we could have? (Those with laces and a separate heel, those with laces that have leather soles, etc.)

6. Could you identify the shoe number when told just one attribute? (Probably not)

7. Is it possible to know all ten attributes and still be unable to identify the shoe's number? (Yes, two shoes might have all ten attributes the same, but still be slightly different)

8. Is this a true statement? The more attributes you know about any object, the easier it is to identify it. (Yes)

XI. Extension

1. The percentage for each of the ten attributes could be tabulated.

2. Instead of using percent, fractions or ratios could be used.

3. Branching keys, or dichotomous keys could be constructed using these or other shoe attributes. (See next page, "How to use a Dichotomous Key.")

Branching

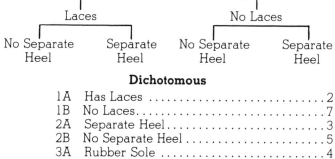

Dichotomous

1A	Has Laces	2
1B	No Laces	7
2A	Separate Heel	3
2B	No Separate Heel	5
3A	Rubber Sole	4
3B	No Rubber Sole	8

4. Measurements of body height could be made, and graphically compared to shoe sizes to see if a correlation exists.

On Your Own Two Feet

NAME _____

SHOE NUMBER	HAS LACES	SEPARATE HEEL	MATERIAL OF SOLE	MATERIAL OF SHOE	NUMBER OF HOLES	NUMBER OF COLORS	MAIN COLOR	LACE COLOR	SHOE TYPE	SIZE
#										
#										
#										
#										
#										
#										
#										
#										
#										
#										
#										
#										

On Your Own Two Feet

SHOE TYPE	TOTAL NUMBER OF TYPE	÷	TOTAL NUMBER OF SHOES IN CLASS	× 100 =	PER CENT OF EACH TYPE
_____	_____	÷	_____	× 100 =	_____
_____	_____	÷	_____	× 100 =	_____
_____	_____	÷	_____	× 100 =	_____
_____	_____	÷	_____	× 100 =	_____
_____	_____	÷	_____	× 100 =	_____
_____	_____	÷	_____	× 100 =	_____
_____	_____	÷	_____	× 100 =	_____
_____	_____	÷	_____	× 100 =	_____

TOTAL NUMBER WITH HEEL	÷	TOTAL NUMBER OF SHOES IN CLASS	× 100 =	PER CENT WITH HEEL
_____	÷	_____	× 100 =	_____

TOTAL NUMBER WITH LACES		TOTAL NUMBER OF SHOES IN CLASS		PER CENT WITH LACES
_____	÷	_____	× 100 =	_____

NOW, GRAPH THE SHOE SIZES IN YOUR CLASS

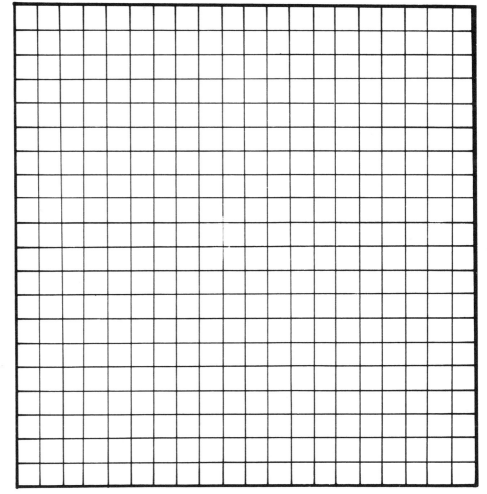

NUMBER

SHOE SIZES

Sorting All Sorts

I. Topic Area
Observation and classification.

II. Introductory Statement
In this classification lesson, students will sort a set of at least ten containers into as many groups of two as possible. The students will group or sort the containers based on characteristics of their own choosing. A guessing game format is used to make this lesson more appealing.

III. Math Skills

Math Skills
a. Sorting
b. Logic
c. Problem Solving

Science Processes
a. Observing
b. Classifying
c. Recording Data

IV. Materials (per group)
A set of at least ten different containers.
Masking tape.

V. Key Question
"How many ways can you sort containers into two groups?"

VI. Background Information
1. The students will probably use the following characteristics (or "rules") to sort their containers: *Color, No Color; Lids, No Lids; Labels, No Labels; Glass, Not Glass; Metal, Not Metal; etc.*

2. A DICHOTOMOUS KEY is a system for classifying elements of a set according to their distinguishing characteristics. In this system the set is first separated into two subsets. Step-by-step separation continues, in like manner, until each element is separate from all others. Thus, such a key can be useful for identifying the name of an object.

3. How to use a Dichotomous Key
   Take any U.S. coin and check it against the information shown at #1 of the key below. You will notice that under each number on the left there are two choices (comparisons): if your object (coin) does not satisfy one, it must satisfy the other. Thus, if your coin is silver in color, read the information shown at #2 of the key. If your coin is smaller than a penny, it is a "DIME." If it is larger than a penny, read the information shown at #3. Continue working down through the key, each time choosing the correct comparison until you arrive at an underlined name.
   The numbers shown at the right indicate the next comparison you must take ("where to go next"). The underlined words are the names. When you arrive at an underlined name, you have successfully "keyed out" your object.

Key to U.S. Coins
1. Silver colored.........................2
   Not silver colored; copper colored....Penny
2. Smaller than penny ....Dime
   Larger than penny.....................3
3. With a picture of a bird 5
   Not with a bird, but with a bison
     (buffalo), a building or a bell 4
4. With a bell (and B. Franklin) ....Half-dollar
   With a "buffalo" or building........Nickel
5. Bird in flying position ....Quarter
   Bird as if standing on branch with
     wings outstretched or clutching
     arrows in one claw...................6
6. With bust of George Washington
     on other side...................Quarter
   Without bust of G. Washington 7
7. With eagle as on National Seal...Half-Dollar
   With eagle in side view, woman's
     figure on other side ....Half-dollar

VII. Management Suggestions
1. The estimated time for this investigation is one or two 45 minute class periods.
2. Make sure that your sets of containers are made of at least three different materials such as glass, metal, plastic, cardboard, etc.
3. Make sure that your sets of containers have at least three different shapes such as cylindrical, rectangular, etc.
4. Try to have some containers with and without lids and labels.
5. Before starting, label each different container with a different letter of the alphabet. Use masking tape to do this.
6. Student groups of 3 or 4 students work well in this activity.

VIII. Procedure
1. Each student group is to obtain a set of at least ten different containers. For identification purposes, each different container must be labeled with a different letter of the alphabet. This can be done with masking tape.
2. One student in the group is to start sorting these containers into two separate piles using a "rule" his or her own choosing...WITHOUT TELLING WHAT THE RULE IS! For example, containers with labels and containers without labels could be one such rule.

3. The other students are to guess what the rule is. When a correct guess is made, the student who guessed correctly gets to sort next. However, before sorting the containers again, a record must be made on the Student Worksheet, page 13, showing the rule used and container types, using alphabet letters, that followed that rule. Example:

RULES	LETTERS
With Lids	B, D, F, I, J
Without Lids	A, C, E, G, H

4. After the record is made, all the containers are placed back into one pile, and a new student starts sorting the containers.

5. At the end of the period, ask each group to report how many different ways they were able to sort their containers into two groups.

IX. What the Students Will Do

1. Sort various containers into two groups based on a rule of their own choosing.

2. Identify the rule being used by other group members to sort the containers.

3. Make a record of each of the different ways their group can sort the containers by listing the individual containers that followed each rule, using the alphabet letters to identify each container.

X. Discussion

1. What kinds of objects are grouped by scientists for study? (Animals, plants, chemicals, stars, clouds, rocks, or practically everything they study)

2. What kinds of objects are grouped or sorted by non-scientists? (Coins, stamp books, pictures, tools, clothing, etc.)

3. What "rules" or characteristics would be useful in grouping or sorting people? (Height, weight, sex, race, marital status, place of birth, age, etc.)

4. What "rules" or characteristics would be useful in grouping or sorting numbers? (Odd or even, multiples, primes, squares, square roots)

5. Why do we sort or classify objects? (For organization, ease in remembering, decision making, etc.)

XI. Extension

1. Venn Diagrams could be made of the container letters, or of sketches of the containers made by the students.

2. A branching key like that shown below could be constructed by the students.

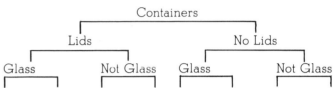

3. Containers could be sorted into three separate groups.

4. A DICHOTOMOUS KEY could be made for the set of containers.

5. Instead of using containers, students could follow the same procedure, only using the CREATURE'S FEATURES student sheet. Students may also want to give each creature a name!

6. A DICHOTOMOUS KEY could also be made for the "CREATURES".

12

Sorting All Sorts

Rules	Letters

Rules	Letters

Rules	Letters

Rules	Letters

Rules	Letters

Rules	Letters

Rules	Letters

Rules	Letters

Creature's Features

A. _____

B. _____

C. _____

D. _____

E. _____

F. _____

G. _____

H. _____

I. _____

J. _____

Creature's Features

Rules   ### Letters

Dichotomous
Key

SUPER SLEUTH

Topic Area
Chemical changes

Introductory Statement
Students will discover the varying characteristics of several substances with somewhat similar appearances.

Science
Observing
Making and testing hypotheses
Classifying
Identifying and controlling variables
Reporting data
Interpreting data

Materials
For the class:
iodine solution (see *Management*)
2 eye droppers
vinegar
source of heat: hot plate (best), candle, bunsen burner
hand magnifiers or microscopes
water
For each student:
small amounts of substances listed
14 - 1 oz. plastic (not paper) portion cups
14 spoons or stirrers
7 tin foil cupcake papers or 10 cm foil squares

Key Question
How can you tell the difference among several white powders?

Background
Substances that look alike may really have chemical compositions that are quite different from one another. To identify a substance, chemical analysis is used, exposing the substance to other substances for which reactions are known. Iodine is used to detect the presence of starch, for example.

Powder number	Drawing of each powder	Vinegar test	Iodine test	Heat test
1 (sugar)	crystal shapes	no visible reaction	no visible reaction	melts, caramelizes, hardens, turns black
2 (salt)	cubic shapes	no visible reaction	no visible reaction	tiny dents in foil
3 (baking soda)	fine powder	bubbles, fizzes	no visible reaction	no visible reaction
4 (corn starch)	fine powder	no visible reaction	turns dark purple	smokes, turns brown, smells like pop corn
5 (plaster of Paris)	fine powder	no visible reaction	no visible reaction	turns gray
6 (white flour)	fine powder	no visible reaction	turns dark purple	turns dark brown, smells like burned toast
Mystery mixture	?	?	?	?

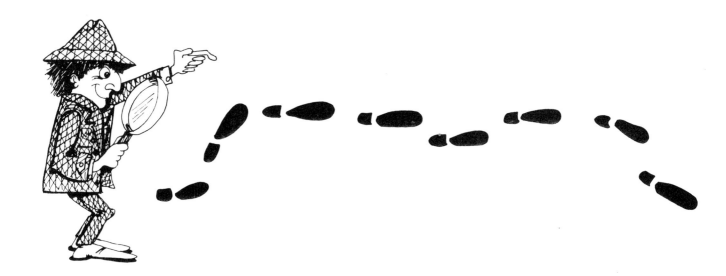

Management

1. Students work well in pairs in this activity.
2. CAUTIONS:
   * This activity should be conducted under close supervision. Use only materials you as a teacher provide.
   * For the heating part of the activity, use safety goggles for all observers and keep a fire extinguisher handy.
   * Iodine will stain clothing, skin, and plastic table tops. Store, use, and dispose of iodine solution with this in mind.
3. Beforehand, prepare iodine solution by mixing one teaspoonful with each cup (8 oz.) of water.
4. Beforehand, prepare the mystery powder by mixing together equal amounts of several of the substances.
5. Keep activity sheets away from the solutions and heat sources.
6. If using a microscope, place a pinch of each substance on a separate slide.
7. Decide the degree of control you wish to have and the approach you think will work best for your group. We have provided instructions for testing one substance at a time; you may prefer to give students all six substances and let them see the reactions to vinegar, for example, before going on to iodine.

Procedure

1. Discuss the Key Question, "How can you tell the difference among several white powders?" Let students share what they already know about the reactions between various common substances, whether white or not.
2. Give each student two plastic and one foil cup. Label the plastic cups "1-V" (vinegar) and "1-I" (iodine); label the foil cup "1."
3. Place a small amount of Powder #1 in each of the three cups. Students examine the substance with magnifier or

microscope and make a detailed drawing of it on the activity sheet.
4. To each 1-V cup add one drop of vinegar. Observe the reaction(s) carefully and record in the appropriate box. Remind students that they may not be able to see all reactions taking place. By saying there is *no visible reactions* they allow for this. They should not smell or taste any substance tested, even if they think they know what it is.
5. Repeat step 4 with the 1-I cup, except to add one drop of iodine solution instead of the vinegar.
6. Predict what will happen when Powder #1 is heated. Heat the foil slowly. Observe the reaction(s) and record. Compare with predictions.
7. Repeat steps 2-6 with each of the other powders through Powder #6.
8. Repeat the steps with the mystery powder. Compare data with results of previous tests for the other substances. Have students try to determine what substances were combined to form the mystery powder.

Discussion

1. Can you identify any of the substances? [Do not emphasize this, since students might try to smell or taste the substances to find out.]
2. For what reasons is it important to be a good observer?
3. Is data from all groups the same? If not, why not?
4. How would you describe the difference between, for example, Powder #1 and Powder #2? [by their differing appearances and their reactions]
5. Give some situations in which chemists might be asked to identify substances as we have today.

Extensions

1. Test other white substances such as laundry powder or talcum powder. Be sure they are non-poisonous.
2. Let students suggest some other tests. [water, red cabbage juice]

Name _____

SUPER SLEUTH

Here are the steps for solving the mystery.

1. Place some of Powder 1 in all 3 cups.
2. Draw what the powder looks like in the box below.
3. Add a drop of vinegar to the first plastic cup. What happens? Record the reaction.
4. Add a drop of iodine solution to the second plastic cup. What happens? Record the reaction.
5. Heat the powder. What happens? Record the reaction.
6. Now do the same with the other powders and the mystery mixture.

Powder number	Drawing of each powder	Vinegar test	Iodine test	Heat test
1				
2				
3				
4				
5				
6				
Mystery mixture				

I think these powders are in the mystery mixture: ____   ____   ____   ____   ____

Explain why you think this. _____

_____

NOTE: DO NOT TRY THESE TESTS AT HOME WITHOUT AN ADULT.

Mini Metric Olympics

I. Topic Area
Estimating and measuring in metric units.

II. Introductory Statement
Students will become familiar with metric units by estimating and measuring in a "Metric Olympic" setting.

III. Math Skills
a. Measuring in Metric Units.

Science Processes
a. Estimating
b. Predicting

IV. Materials (per class)
2-3 paper plates or pie pans
3-5 paper or plastic drinking straws
2 bags of marbles
3 meter sticks and meter tapes
cotton puff balls
large sponge
large mixing bowl or bucket
liter measuring set
centimeter graph paper
balance scale with weights
Student Worksheets

V. Key Question
"How closely can you match your estimate and your actual measurement in metric units?"

VII. Management Suggestions
1. Establish fair ground rules ahead of time.
2. Be consistent in guiding rules that determine fairness in measurement. For Example: Do I get a practice turn?
3. Measure to the nearest whole unit.
4. Teacher needs to announce when teams will rotate to the next station.
5. Estimated time to complete activity is two (2) fifty minute class periods.

VIII. Procedure
1. Work in small groups (5) including a team captain.
2. There are a total of six stations with a different task at each station. Each station should have a task card with complete instructions and materials available. Each group is assigned to one station.
3. Each captain may read the instructions to his team. It is extremely important that *before* each activity begins, each student estimates and records his/her estimate on his/her student score sheet. Captains should check all members on the team before beginning any activity.
4. After each team member performs the activity, he/she measures and records his/her actual length, mass, volume or area.

IX. What the Students Will Do
After all the stations have been completed by all teams, each student should find the score, which is the difference between the estimates and the actual measurement for each event. This should be entered in the last column. Then each student totals the numbers in the score column. The winner is the one with the lowest score. You may wish to discuss how a low score shows accuracy.

Awards may be presented to the winners. There are forms in the student worksheet section which may be duplicated for this purpose.

XI. Extension
You may wish to use one or both of the self-explanatory extended activities: Metric Scavenger Hunt or Mini-Metric Olympics II. Mini-Metric Olympics II requires the computation of percent of error and is appropriate for the upper grades.

Following are other investigations that require estimation and measurement:
a. How many liters of water will fill your bathtub? Draw a cartoon and record your data.
b. Select five or more containers of assorted sizes and shapes. Can you arrange them in order from least to greatest and predict their volume accurately? Make a diagram and table of your results.
c. Select five or more objects of various sizes and shapes. Can you arrange them from lightest to heaviest and estimate their mass accurately? Organize and illustrate your data.
d. Estimate the distance of a trip to school and back home in metric units. Draw a map to scale that illustrates how far you walk or ride to school. You may choose to do this with a partner and do a combined map so that you can make comparisons.

Event

Athlete

19

Fill in the year.

Event

Athlete

19

Olympic Symbol

Five interlocking rings represent the five major continents of the world. Their colors in order from left to right are: blue, yellow, black, green, and red.

These colors are special because at least one of them appears in the flag of every nation of the world. These colorful rings are joined together to remind us of the sporting friendship of all mankind.

History: Ancient Games

Traditionally the accepted date of the first Olympiad is 776 B.C. but there is reasonable certainty that they were held considerably earlier than that. These festivities were held in Olympia, Greece where a stadium and a temple to Zeus were built. On selected occasions "a day of games" was held to honor a god or a dead hero. Only males were allowed to participate and events originally included a foot race, also called the stadium race, a long distance foot race, wrestling, and the pentathlon which was a combination of five events. The ancient games ceased to take place after 392 A.D. because they were viewed by Christians as a pagan ritual.

The Olympic Motto:

Citius, Altius, Fortius

from the Latin meaning swifter, higher, stronger. These words are used to build healthy attitudes and winning spirits in preparation for competition.

The Olympic Flame:

The Olympic Flame is lighted by the Olympic torch during the opening ceremonies. The flame is a symbol of peace and is lit first in the temple of Zeus in Olympia. Thousands of relay runners from many countries then carry it to the stadium of the city hosting the games. The flame is passed by hand from one runner to the next.

Modern Olympic Games

Credit for the revival of the Olympic Games goes to Pierre de Coubertin, a French baron who felt strongly about bringing together representatives from many nations for the purpose of peaceful competition. He posed these words that now make up the Olympic creed: "The most important thing in the Olympic Games is not to win but to take part, just as the most important thing in life is not the triumph but the struggle. The essential thing is not to have conquered but to have fought well." With respect and honor to Greece, the land of the original games, the first modern games were held in Athens in 1896 where nine countries came together.

The 1988 Olympic Games were held in Seoul, South Korea where 161 countries competed in 23 Olympic sports. Winners in each event earned gold, silver and bronze medals for their performances. Each athlete made this pledge:

We swear that we will take part in these Olympic Games in the true spirit of sportsmanship and that we will respect and abide by the rules which govern them for the glory of the sport and the honor of our country.

MINI-METRIC OLYMPICS

COMPETITOR _____

TEAM CAPTAIN _____

EVENT	ESTIMATE	ACTUAL	SCORE (DIFFERENCE)
1. PAPER PLATE DISCUS	_____ cm	_____ cm	_____
2. PAPER STRAW JAVELIN	_____ cm	_____ cm	_____
3. COTTON BALL SHOT PUT	_____ cm	_____ cm	_____
4. RIGHT HANDED MARBLE GRAB	_____ g	_____ g	_____
5. LEFT-HANDED SPONGE SQUEEZE	_____ ml	_____ ml	_____
6. BIG FOOT CONTEST	_____ cm^2	_____ cm^2	_____

TOTAL _____

1 26 51 76 1 26 51 76
2 27 52 77 2 27 52 77
3 28 53 78 3 28 53 78
4 29 54 79 4 29 54 79
5 30 55 80 5 30 55 80
6 31 56 81 6 31 56 81
7 32 57 82 7 32 57 82
8 33 58 83 8 33 58 83
9 34 59 84 9 34 59 84
10 35 60 85 10 35 60 85
11 36 61 86 11 36 61 86
12 37 62 87 12 37 62 87
13 38 63 88 13 38 63 88
14 39 64 89 14 39 64 89
15 40 65 90 15 40 65 90
16 41 66 91 16 41 66 91
17 42 67 92 17 42 67 92
18 43 68 93 18 43 68 93
19 44 69 94 19 44 69 94
20 45 70 95 20 45 70 95
21 46 71 96 21 46 71 96
22 47 72 97 22 47 72 97
23 48 73 98 23 48 73 98
24 49 74 99 24 49 74 99
25 50 75 100 METER 25 50 75 100 METER

PAPER STRAW JAVELIN THROW

PAPER STRAW THROW

1. Place feet on starting line. Throw "javelin". (One throw only.)

2. Estimate the distance (in cm) that you threw the "javelin." Record.

3. Measure distance from starting line to the position of the "javelin." Record.

MINI-METRIC OLYMPICS
TASK CARD

PAPER PLATE DISCUS

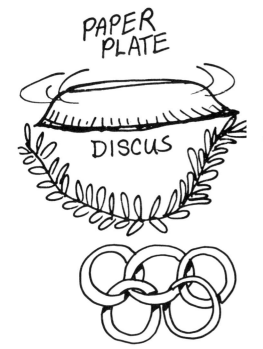

PAPER PLATE

DISCUS

1. Place feet on starting line. Throw the "discus" (one throw only)

2. Estimate the distance (in cm) that you threw the "discus." Record.

3. Measure distance from starting line to the position of the paper plate. Record.

MINI-METRIC OLYMPICS
TASK CARD

COTTON BALL SHOT PUT

1. Place feet on starting line. Throw the "cotton ball shot." (One throw only.)

2. Estimate the distance (in cm) that you put the "shot." Record.

3. Measure distance from starting line to the position of the cotton ball. Record.

RIGHT-HANDED MARBLE GRAB

1. With the right hand only, grab a fistful of marbles from the container.

   Place marbles on a balance scale.

2. Estimate (in grams) the mass of marbles you grabbed in your right hand. Record.

3. Measure the mass of the marbles. Record.

LEFT-HANDED SPONGE SQUEEZE

1. Have sponge soaking in large bucket of water. Observe.

2. Squeeze sponge into separate container. (one squeeze only)

3. Estimate the amount of water (in ml) you squeezed out of the sponge. Record.

4. Measure water squeezed. Record.

MINI-METRIC OLYMPICS
TASK CARD

BIG FOOT WAS HERE!

1. Remove one shoe. Trace around your foot on square centimeter graph paper.

2. Estimate in square cm the area of your foot print. Record.

3. Figure the area of your foot print. Record.

MINI-METRIC Olympics
TASK CARD

Mini-Metric Olympics Awards

PAPER STRAW THROW

SPONGE SQUEEZE

PAPER PLATE DISCUS

BIG FOOT

COTTON BALL SHOTPUT

RIGHT HANDED MARBLE GRAB

MiniMetric Olympics II

$$\frac{Error}{Actual} \times 100 = \% \text{ of } ERROR$$

EVENT	ESTIMATE	ACTUAL	ERROR	% ERROR	SCORE
LENGTH 1. HAND SPAN	mm				
2. ARM SPAN (tip to tip)	cm				
3. STEADY STRIDE	cm				
MASS 1. WALLET	g				
2. PENCIL	g				
3. PERSONAL ITEM (FREE CHOICE)	g				
4. BODY WEIGHT	Kg				
VOLUME 1. PEN CAP	ml				
2. PAPER CUP	ml				
3. YOUR FIST	ml				
4. BLOCK OF WOOD	ml				
AREA 1. SHEET OF PAPER	cm²				
2. CLASSROOM CEILING	cm²				
3. FOOTBALL FIELD	m²				
4. DESK TOP	cm²				

METRIC SCAVENGER HUNT

Try to find objects of these lengths	Name of Object	Actual Measurement	Difference
1. 40 cm			
2. 87 cm			
3. 3 cm			
4. 1 m			
5. 31 cm			
6. 1.5 m			
7. 65 mm			
8. 240 mm			
9. 28 cm			
10. 2 mm			
		☆ Total Differences ☆	

COOL IT!

I. Topic Area
Interpreting Data

II. Introductory Statement
Students will measure the length of time it takes hot water to cool in a styrofoam cup compared to the length of time it takes hot water to cool in a tin can. Upon completion of the activity, students will be able to determine which material is a better insulator for liquids, tin or styrofoam.

III. Math Skills
a. Observing
b. Measuring
c. Recording Data
d. Interpreting Data
e. Generalizing

Science Processes
a. Collecting Data
b. Comparing Data
c. Drawing Conclusions

IV. Materials (per group)
1 styrofoam cup
1 clean tin can of the same volume
2 Celsius thermometers
1 stopwatch
1 liter container
Anything that will heat water to 75 degrees Celsius

V. Key Question
"In which container will the hot water retain its heat longer? Why?

VII. Management Suggestions
1. Have the students work in small groups.
2. Provide each group with the appropriate materials.
3. Estimated time: One 45 minute period.
4. Practice reading thermometers.
5. Record to the nearest degree.

VIII. Procedure
1. Heat water to at least 75 degrees Celsius.
2. Students will pour 200 ml of water with a temperature of 75 degrees Celsius or higher into each

container as quickly as possible. They must be careful not to touch the water.
3. Students will insert a Celsius thermometer into each container.
4. Students begin taking readings as soon as the thermometers stop rising and they record the temperature.
5. A student starts a stopwatch at this point.
6. Students take and record readings on the thermometers in one minute intervals.
7. Students record the results each minute for both thermometers.
8. They must record the temperature at its highest point first and then continue at one minute intervals for 15 minutes.
9. After completing the temperature data record, the students construct a line graph showing the temperatures of the water in each container.
10. Students record the results on the same graph using two different colors, one color for each container's results.
11. The results of the graph are then studied.

IX. What the Students Will Do
1. Measure the temperature of water using Celsius thermometers.
2. Record temperatures at one minute intervals for fifteen minutes.
3. Construct a line graph.

X. Discussion
Encourage the students to draw conclusions about the relationship between the time it took the water to cool in one container compared to the other container.

XI. Extension
Instead of using only two containers, use several kinds (tin, plastic, glass, etc.).

COOL IT!

Which container will retain its heat the longest? _____

TEMPERATURE RECORD

TIME IN MINUTES	STYROFOAM CUP	TIN CAN
STARTING TEMP.		
1		
2		
3		
4		
5		
6		
7		
8		
9		
10		
11		
12		
13		
14		
15		

Start recording temperatures as soon as the thermometers stop rising.

STYROFOAM CUP

TIN CAN

Record the temperatures every minute for 15 minutes.

Make a line graph to show the rate of cooling for each container.

TEMPERATURE C°

85°
80°
75°
70°
65°
60°
55°
50°
45°
40°
35°
30°
25°
20°

0 1 2 3 4 5 6 7 8 9 10 11 12 13 14 15

MINUTES

Hot Stuff

I. Topic Area
Measuring Temperature

II. Introductory Statement
Students will discover which materials make the best insulators.

III. Math Skills
a. Measuring Temperature
b. Graphing

Science Processes
a. Observing
b. Measuring Temperature
c. Recording Data
d. Interpreting Data

IV. Materials (per group)
Timer for each group
Hot water (75° C.)
Container to measure 300 ml of water
Aluminum soda pop cans with pull-off tabs
Deeper cans such as those used for fruit and vegetable juices
Celsius thermometer for each group
Materials to be used as insulators (four or more of the following): sawdust, cotton, shredded paper, vermiculite, fiber glass, sand, foam plastic (such as that used for packaging), and air.

V. Key Question
"Which insulation material will keep the water hot the longest?

VII. Management Suggestions
1. Have different groups work on different insulators and compile the results for the class.
2. Use three students in each group—one for timing, one for reading the temperature and one for recording.
3. Estimated time: one or two 45 minute class periods.

VIII. Procedure
Instructions for setting up insulated cans.
1. Using the insulator you want to test, place at least 2-3 cm (one inch) of material in the bottom of the outside container.
2. Set the inside container on this, centering it in the outside container.
3. Pack the space in between with the same insulation.

Procedure for completing the investigation.
1. Pour 300 ml of water with a temperature of about 75° Celsius into the aluminum can.
2. Insert the thermometer into the water.
3. As soon as the temperature reaches 70° C., start the timer.
4. Record the temperature every minute for fifteen minutes.
5. Have students graph the results.

IX. What the Students Will Do
1. Select various insulators for testing.
2. Accurately measure 300 ml of water for testing.
3. Record temperatures every minute for 15 minutes.
4. Graph temperatures for each insulator.

X. Discussion Questions
1. Which material let the water cool off fastest?
2. Which material kept the water warm the longest?
3. Which material is the best insulator?

XI. Extension
More capable students with more time could test more than one material. Some may wish to extend the investigation to find the best possible insulator.

HOT STUFF

What makes the best insulator?

As soon as the water temperature reaches 70°C, Record the temperature every minute for 15 minutes.

Insulator	TIME IN MINUTES														
	1	2	3	4	5	6	7	8	9	10	11	12	13	14	15

Insulator List
sawdust   cotton
shredded paper
vermiculite
fiberglass   foam
sand
air   plastic

Outside Container

THERMOMETER

Aluminum Can

1. Pick an insulator.
2. Put 1 inch in bottom of outside container.
3. Set Aluminum Can on insulator and center it in outside container.
4. Pack remaining space with the same insulation
5. Put 300 ml of 75°C water in aluminum can.
6. As soon as the water reaches 70°C, start the timer.

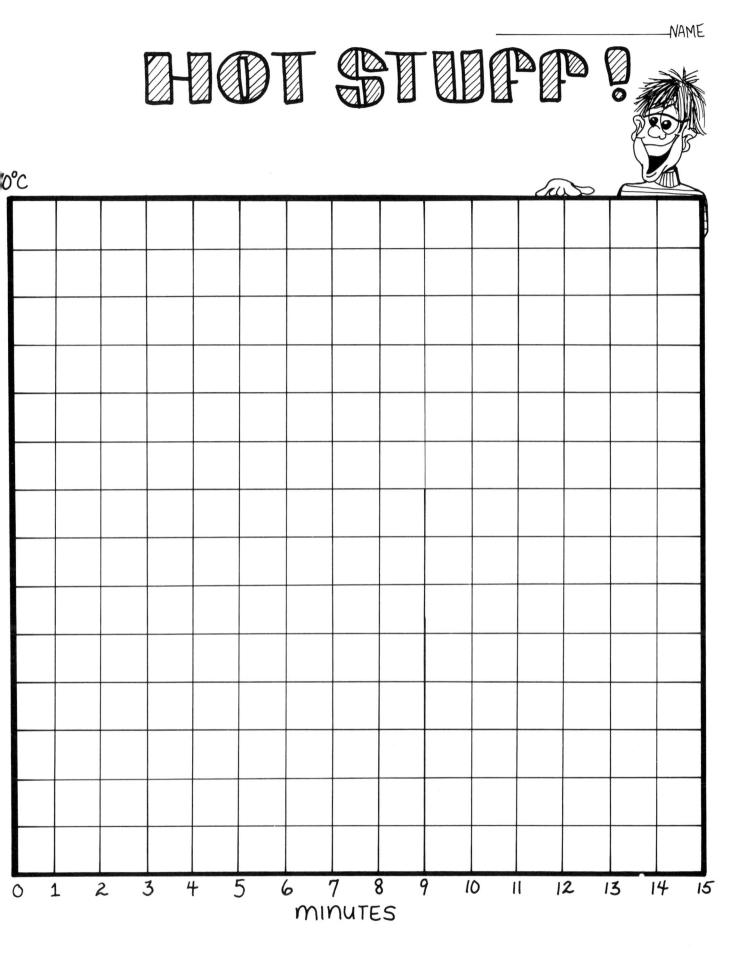

HOT STUFF!

_____ NAME

0°C

minutes
0 1 2 3 4 5 6 7 8 9 10 11 12 13 14 15

Corny Comparison

I. Topic Area
Measurement of volume

II. Introductory Statement
Students will practice measuring volume in metric units. Students will find the ratio of popped to un-popped popcorn.

III. Math Skills

Math Skills
a. Measuring Volume in Metric Units
b. Determining Ratios

Science Processes
a. Measuring
b. Predicting
c. Controlling Variables
d. Recording Data
e. Generalizing

IV. Materials (per class)
Popcorn popper - more than one may be helpful
A supply of two brands of popcorn
Oil
Graduated cylinders or cups that measure in milliliters, one set for each group
Student Worksheet

V. Key Question
"How much will the volume of popcorn expand when it is popped?"

VI. Background Information
To find the ratio of popped to unpopped corn, measure each using the graduated cylinder or cups. For example, if the investigation using 130 ml of corn produces 950 ml of popped corn, the ratio of popped to unpopped is 950:130. However, it is more convenient to work with 1, so we divide both numbers by 130 and get the ratio 7.3:1. We interpret this to say that the volume of popped corn is 7.3 times the volume of the unpopped corn.

VII. Management Suggestions
1. Have an adult supervise the popping of the corn.
2. Have everyone make their estimate before the first group pops their popcorn.
3. Alternate between brands to minimize differences in conditions.
4. Estimated time: two to four 45 minute class periods.
5. The class will divide into eight groups and each group will perform one popcorn popping experiment.

6. Assign the groups as follows:

Group		Volume of Popcorn	Volume of Oil
1	Brand A	70 ml.	20 ml.
2		100 ml.	30 ml.
3		130 ml.	40 ml.
4		160 ml.	50 ml.
5	Brand B	70 ml.	20 ml.
6		100 ml.	30 ml.
7		130 ml.	40 ml.
8		160 ml.	50 ml.

IX. What the Students Will Do
1. Each student will first estimate the volume of the popped corn for his or her particular group.
2. Each group will pop their popcorn and measure the volume, then make a record of the results.
3. Each group will calculate the ratio of the popped corn to the unpopped corn.
4. All groups will share their data.

X. Discussion
1. How much did the popcorn increase in volume?
2. Who came the closest to predicting the correct volume?
3. Compare the ratio of the predicted and actual results, popped to unpopped corn.
4. Which brand gave the best results?
5. Which brand is the most expensive?
6. Is the difference in cost worth it?

XI. Extension
1. Students could determine the cost of a liter of popped corn for each brand and make a direct comparison.
2. Students could determine in what volume they would like to sell popcorn (1 liter, 1.5 liter, etc.) and then determine how much popcorn they would need to buy to sell a hundred bags of popcorn.
3. If students do (2) above, they could also compute the cost per bag of the popcorn alone or the popcorn and the oil. This still ignores the cost of labor and electricity.

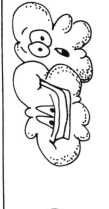

Corn Comparison

BRAND A.

ml corn	70	100	130	160
ml oil	20	30	40	50
ESTIMATED VOLUME POPPED CORN				
ACTUAL VOLUME				
RATIO OF THE VOLUME OF POPPED / UNPOPPED				

BRAND B.

ml corn	70	100	130	160
ml oil	20	30	40	50
ESTIMATED VOLUME POPPED CORN				
ACTUAL VOLUME				
RATIO OF THE VOLUME OF POPPED / UNPOPPED				

Please compare the amount of popped corn to unpopped corn. About how many times did the volume of unpopped popcorn expand when popped? _____

Please write a sentence to explain what you discovered.

_____

Weight Watchers

I. **Topic Area**

Estimating and measuring mass.

II. **Introductory Statement**

Weight Watchers is an activity that requires students to estimate and measure mass.

III. **Math Skills**
   a. Measuring
   b. Estimating
   c. Computing Ratio and Percent (optional)
   d. Using Calculators (optional)
   e. Averaging

Science Processes
   a. Observing
   b. Measuring
   c. Predicting and Estimating
   d. Recording Data

IV. **Materials (per group)**

Golf ball
Marble
Wooden block that weighs less than, but is larger than the golf ball
Tennis ball
Ping Pong ball
Clay ball
Equal arm balance with Metric mass set
Student Worksheet

V. **Key Question**

"Can you order the objects from heaviest to lightest using only visual clues?"

VI. **Background Information**

The difference between the estimated mass and the actual mass, divided by the actual mass, multiplied by 100 equals the percent of error.

$$\frac{\text{difference}}{\text{actual mass}} \times 100 = \% \text{ of error}$$

Examples:

Item	Estimated Mass in Grams	Actual Mass in Grams	Percent of Error
Golf Ball	20	35	43%
Marble	15	10	50%

Golf Ball

Actual mass	35
Estimated mass	− 20
Absolute difference	15

```
        .428      Rounded off
Actual mass  35)15.000   equals .43
        14 0
         1 00     .43 × 100 = 43%
           70
          300
          280
           20
```

Marble

Estimated mass	15
Actual mass	− 10
	5

```
            .50
Actual mass  10)5.00    .50 × 100 = 50%
             5 0
```

VII. **Management Suggestions**

This activity can be done in small groups or in a whole group activity. The activity can be done in one 45 minute class period.

VIII. **Procedure**

Collect all the necessary materials mentioned in the Materials Section IV. Give each student a copy of the worksheet. Place the objects where all the students can see them. Go through the worksheet step by step with the students. It might be helpful to make an overhead transparency of the worksheet and explain to the students before you begin what they will be doing.

IX. **What the Students Will Do**
   1. The students will order the objects from the heaviest to the lightest visually and record their guess.
   2. The students will estimate the mass of each object.
   3. The students can work in small groups and weigh the objects while the rest of the class watches.
   4. All the students will record the actual mass in grams.
   5. Students will find and record the difference between the actual mass and estimated mass.

Students may stop at this point. If the teacher feels that students are capable, the teacher may have the students continue to fill in the chart. This is a good opportunity to have students use calculators.

Optional
   6. Have students find their average error. A small prize could be awarded to the student with the lowest average error.
   7. Have students find the ratio.
   8. Have students convert the ratio to a decimal.
   9. Have students compute the percent of error.

X. **Discussion**
   1. Is there a way the estimations can be checked for accuracy?
   2. Can you estimate the mass of the objects in grams and then find the actual mass in grams?
   3. Discuss with the students what their rationale for ordering the items from heaviest to lightest was.

XI. **Extension**

Provide each student with a chart that has all the items left out. Let the students choose 6 items of which they would like to estimate the mass and then continue on with the mathematical calculations.

MATH + SCIENCE: A SOLUTION

© 1987 AIMS Education Foundation

Weight Watchers

Golf Ball

Marble

Wooden Block

Tennis Ball

Ping Pong Ball

Clay Ball

1. Look at the 6 items. List them in order from heaviest to lightest:

1._____
2._____
3._____
4._____
5._____
6._____

2. Next, estimate their mass (grams).
3. Weigh to find their actual mass.
4. Determine the error of your guess.
5. Compute the percent of error.

Item	Estimated Mass in Grams	Actual Mass in Grams	Error (Difference)	Ratio Difference/Actual	Decimal Diff. ÷ Actual	Percent of Error Decimal x 100
Golf Ball						
Marble						
Wooden Block						
Tennis Ball						
Ping Pong Ball						
Clay Ball						
	Average Error			Average Percent of Error		

Weight Watchers

Sketch →
the
6 objects

[ ]

1. LOOK AT 6 ITEMS. LIST THEM IN ORDER FROM HEAVIEST TO LIGHTEST.

2. NOW ESTIMATE THEIR MASS (grams).
3. WEIGH AND FIND THEIR ACTUAL MASS.
4. DETERMINE THE ERROR OF YOUR GUESS.
5. FIND THE RATIO.
6. COMPUTE THE PER CENT OF ERROR.

1. _____
2. _____
3. _____
4. _____
5. _____
6. _____

ITEM	ESTIMATED MASS IN GRAMS	ACTUAL MASS IN GRAMS	ERROR (DIFFERENCE)	RATIO: $\frac{DIFFERENCE}{ACTUAL}$	DECIMAL DIFF. ÷ ACTUAL	PER CENT OF ERROR DECIMAL X 100

AVERAGE ERROR [ ]

AVERAGE PER CENT OF ERROR [ ]

SECOND GUESSING

I. Topic Area
Estimating and Recording Data

II. Introductory Statement
Students will compete to see which students are able to estimate time accurately.

III. Math Skills
a. Estimation
b. Ratio
c. Percent
d. Timing

Science Processes
a. Estimating
b. Recording Data

IV. Materials
Clock or watches with second hand or a stop watch
Recording sheets
Student Worksheet

V. Key Question
"Who can guess when 30 seconds have passed?" Have students close their eyes and raise their hands when they guess 30 seconds have passed.

VII. Management Suggestions
1. Estimated time: one 45 minute class period.
2. You will need one time piece for every two students. (The classroom clock may be used if it has a second hand)
3. Students need to be familiar with ratio in whatever form you plan to use.
4. If the investigation is done in a learning center, only one stop watch is needed.
5. Calculators can be used for the division, if the teacher desires.

VIII. Procedure
1. Students will work in pairs to estimate time.
2. One student will act as the timer; the other as the estimator. (Students must switch roles so that all students have a chance to do both.)
3. The timer selects a time period, such as 60 seconds, and tells the estimator to raise his/her hand when he thinks 60 seconds are up. The timer records the actual time period in the table under the column "Time Estimate".
4. The timer may then tell the estimator how many seconds actually passed.
5. The estimator should repeat the exercise (Trial 2) trying to estimate this same time period.
6. Repeat using other time periods and do each time period at least twice.

IX. What the Students Will Do
1. Students will estimate time. One student estimates a given length of time (with his back to the clock) while the other student monitors the actual time.
2. Students will find the difference between the estimate and the actual time passed. This is called "the error of estimate".
3. Students will find the ratio of the error to the time period.
4. Students will express the ratio as a decimal and then as a percent.

X. Discussion
1. How well did you estimate? Did your estimates improve with practice or did they become poorer?
2. How were you able to make a fairly accurate estimate?
3. Are some people better at estimating than others?
4. What methods are best for estimating?
5. Why are clocks and watches needed to measure time?

XI. Extension
1. For grades 7-8, do the percent error. Graph the results.

WHO EVER SAID TIME FLIES?!!

SECOND GUESSING

WHO EVER SAID TIME FLIES?!!

TRIAL NUMBER	TIME PERIOD (SECONDS)	TIME ESTIMATE (ACTUAL SECONDS)	ERROR OF ESTIMATE	RATIO (ERROR/TIME PERIOD)	DECIMAL (ERROR ÷ TIME PERIOD)	% of ERROR (DECIMAL × 100)

Chaotic Computing!

I. Topic Area
This is a study of the effect of distractions on studying.

II. Introductory Statement
This is a study of the effect of distractions on studying.

III. Math Skills
a. Timing
b. Whole Number Computations

Science Processes
a. Recording Data
b. Controlling Variables

IV. Materials
Student Worksheets
Stop watch or clock with second hand

V. Key Question
"Do I study better with or without distractions?"

VI. Background Information
The control of variables is an extremely important concept in scientific experimentation. A *variable* is any factor that can change or cause a change in an experiment. Scientists seek to control all variables except the one being tested. For example, if we want to know the effect of distraction on problem solving, distraction is the variable we want to study. Other variables such as time of day, difficulty of the problems, or method of distraction must be controlled. In this way, if we find a difference in computational ability, we can be fairly certain that it was caused only by the distraction and not a different factor.

VII. Management Suggestions
1. Discuss the type of problems that will be worked.
2. Review subtraction of time with the students before beginning.

3. If your room doesn't have a clock with a second hand, you can write the beginning times on the chalkboard. As the students finish, have them raise their hands and write the ending times on the board.
4. Note: Some students will work better with distraction.

IX. What the Students Will Do
1. a. Students will work the 20 problems in Set A without distraction.
   b. They will record the beginning times on their worksheets.
   c. As they finish, each will quietly write down the ending time.
   d. Each will compute the length of time required.
2. a. Each student will find a partner to do Set B.
   b. One student will read the list of numbers on the student worksheet as many times as necessary. This will provide a distraction to the student working the problems.
   c. Students will compute and record the length of time required to complete the set of problems.
   d. Partners will switch places and repeat steps a, b, and c.
3. Correct the problems and record the number correct on the tables.

X. Discussion Questions
1. Which problem set did you complete faster?
2. On which problems were you most accurate?
3. What seems to be affected more—speed or accuracy?
4. What do your results suggest about your ability to study with or without distraction?
5. Would we have different results if we reversed the investigation? (working with distraction first; then working without distraction).

Chaotic Computing!　　　 ## Chaotic Computing!

5 +8 **13**	11 −4 **7**	137 −49 **88**	135 +87 **222**	12 −3 **9**	152 −74 **78**	8 +7 **15**	193 +89 **282**
8 −6 **2**	321 −57 **264**	5 +27 **32**	748 +77 **825**	231 −78 **153**	837 +68 **905**	4 −1 **3**	29 +3 **32**
69 +32 **101**	424 +386 **810**	145 −126 **19**	17 −9 **8**	127 −108 **19**	58 +43 **101**	473 +237 **710**	13 −7 **6**
13 +97 **110**	403 −304 **99**	573 −477 **96**	7977 +8744 **16,721**	743 −648 **95**	302 −203 **99**	48 +9 **57**	8723 +7999 **16,722**
5273 −3827 **1446**	62,785 −38,068 **24,717**	142,348 +161,764 **304,112**	557,863 −456,954 **100,909**	6382 −4525 **1857**	71,523 −42,634 **28,889**	174,875 +131,239 **306,114**	573,641 −472,732 **100,909**

　26.　　　　27.

Chaotic Computing!　　　 ## Chaotic Computing!

8 x9 **72**	54 ÷ 9 = **6**	6 x7 **42**	24 ÷ 8 = **3**	9 x5 **45**	42 ÷ 7 = **6**	3 x8 **24**	72 ÷ 8 = **9**
32 x4 **128**	831 x6 **4986**	**72 r 4** 6) 436	4200 ÷ 60 = **70**	42 x3 **126**	613 x8 **4904**	**61 r 5** 8) 493	3500 ÷ 70 = **50**
236 x9 **2124**	903 x5 **4515**	**40 r 3** 5) 203	9600 ÷ 10 = **960**	623 x9 **5607**	309 x5 **1545**	**60 r 2** 5) 302	4500 ÷ 100 = **45**
396 x32 **12,672**	765 x29 **22,185**	308 x13 **4004**	**331 r 22** 23) 7635	693 x23 **15,939**	576 x92 **52,992**	803 x31 **24,893**	**210 r 15** 32) 6735
306 x604 **184,824**	813 x 134 **108,942**	496 x109 **54,064**	6934 x943 **6,538,762**	406 x603 **244,818**	314 x138 **43,332**	964 x901 **868,564**	3964 x349 **1,383,436**

　28.　　　　29.

Chaotic Computing!

READ THESE NUMBERS TO YOUR PARTNER TO DISTRACT THEM

TABLE 1
SET A   (WITHOUT DISTRACTION)

TIME BEGUN	TIME FINISHED	TIME TAKEN	NUMBER CORRECT

TABLE 2
SET B   (WITH DISTRACTON)

TIME BEGUN	TIME FINISHED	TIME TAKEN	NUMBER CORRECT

10	17
3	15
5	8
8	15
6	6
9	18
1	9
4	11
7	1
2	13
12	4
20	19
17	4
15	14
14	6
18	13
13	2
16	19
19	30
2	45
12	7
5	3
20	1
3	13
7	6

10..3...5..8..
6..9..1..
4..7..2

Chaotic Computing!

$$\begin{array}{r} 5 \\ +8 \\ \hline \end{array} \qquad \begin{array}{r} 11 \\ -4 \\ \hline \end{array} \qquad \begin{array}{r} 137 \\ -49 \\ \hline \end{array} \qquad \begin{array}{r} 135 \\ +87 \\ \hline \end{array}$$

$$\begin{array}{r} 8 \\ -6 \\ \hline \end{array} \qquad \begin{array}{r} 321 \\ -57 \\ \hline \end{array} \qquad \begin{array}{r} 5 \\ +27 \\ \hline \end{array} \qquad \begin{array}{r} 748 \\ +77 \\ \hline \end{array}$$

$$\begin{array}{r} 69 \\ +32 \\ \hline \end{array} \qquad \begin{array}{r} 424 \\ +386 \\ \hline \end{array} \qquad \begin{array}{r} 145 \\ -126 \\ \hline \end{array} \qquad \begin{array}{r} 17 \\ -9 \\ \hline \end{array}$$

$$\begin{array}{r} 13 \\ +97 \\ \hline \end{array} \qquad \begin{array}{r} 403 \\ -304 \\ \hline \end{array} \qquad \begin{array}{r} 573 \\ -477 \\ \hline \end{array} \qquad \begin{array}{r} 7977 \\ +8744 \\ \hline \end{array}$$

$$\begin{array}{r} 5273 \\ -3827 \\ \hline \end{array} \qquad \begin{array}{r} 62{,}785 \\ -38{,}068 \\ \hline \end{array} \qquad \begin{array}{r} 142{,}348 \\ +161{,}764 \\ \hline \end{array} \qquad \begin{array}{r} 557{,}863 \\ -456{,}954 \\ \hline \end{array}$$

Chaotic Computing!

```
  12          152           8          193
  −3          −74          +7          +89
```

```
 231          837           4           29
 −78          +68          −1           +3
```

```
 127           58         473           13
−108          +43        +237           −7
```

```
 743          302          48         8723
−648         −203          +9        +7999
```

```
 6382       71,523     174,875      573,641
−4525      −42,634    +131,239     −472,732
```

Chaotic Computing!

$$\begin{array}{r} 8 \\ \times 9 \\ \hline \end{array}$$

$54 \div 9 =$

$$\begin{array}{r} 6 \\ \times 7 \\ \hline \end{array}$$

$24 \div 8 =$

$$\begin{array}{r} 32 \\ \times 4 \\ \hline \end{array}$$

$$\begin{array}{r} 831 \\ \times 6 \\ \hline \end{array}$$

$6\overline{)436}$

$4200 \div 60 =$

$$\begin{array}{r} 236 \\ \times 9 \\ \hline \end{array}$$

$$\begin{array}{r} 903 \\ \times 5 \\ \hline \end{array}$$

$5\overline{)203}$

$9600 \div 10 =$

$$\begin{array}{r} 396 \\ \times 32 \\ \hline \end{array}$$

$$\begin{array}{r} 765 \\ \times 29 \\ \hline \end{array}$$

$$\begin{array}{r} 308 \\ \times 13 \\ \hline \end{array}$$

$23\overline{)7635}$

$$\begin{array}{r} 306 \\ \times 604 \\ \hline \end{array}$$

$$\begin{array}{r} 813 \\ \times 134 \\ \hline \end{array}$$

$$\begin{array}{r} 496 \\ \times 109 \\ \hline \end{array}$$

$$\begin{array}{r} 6934 \\ \times 943 \\ \hline \end{array}$$

Chaotic Computing!

```
  9
 x5          42 ÷ 7 =
```

```
  3
 x8          72 ÷ 8 =
```

```
 42     613
 x3     x8        8 | 493        3500 ÷ 70 =
```

```
623     309
 x9     x5        5 | 302        4500 ÷ 100 =
```

```
693      576      803
x23      x92      x31       32 | 6735
```

```
406           314           964          3964
x603          x138          x901         x349
```

50

"It's Simply Marbleous"

I. Topic Area
Interpreting Data and Controlling Variables

II. Introductory Statement
A marble will be rolled down an inclined plane several times from different heights. Upon the completion of this activity, students will be able to describe the relationship between the slope of an incline plane and the distance an object will roll.

III. Math Skills
a. Averaging
b. Graphing
c. Measuring
d. Adding

Science Processes
a. Collecting Data
b. Predicting/Estimating
c. Observing
d. Measuring
e. Recording Data
f. Interpreting Data
g. Controlling Variables

IV. Materials (per group)
16 books (each with a spine about 2cm in width)
2 meter sticks
1 marble
1 metric tape measure
masking tape
Student Worksheet

V. Key Question
"How does the slope of an incline plane affect the distance a marble will roll?"

VI. Background Information
Generally, the steeper the slope, the farther the marble will roll. Eventually, the height of the slope will become so steep that the marble will not continue to roll as far as it did previously. This is due to the fact that the forward motion of the marble is absorbed into the floor.

VII. Management Suggestions
1. Estimated time: One 45 minute period.
2. Demonstrate this activity to the students by setting up the inclined plane.
3. Find a fairly open area which has smooth carpeting or use a sheet spread on the floor. The texture of the surface on which a marble rolls will be a factor in how far it rolls.
4. Attach about 5 cm of masking tape to the metric rulers at the top and bottom so there is a separation wide enough for a marble to roll down.
5. Place one book with a 2 cm spine on the floor. From the edge of the book spine mark a baseline 88 cm with a piece of tape.
6. Place the meter sticks on top of the book so that the ends of the meter sticks meet the 88 cm tape mark on the floor.

7. Practice gently placing the marble in the groove and releasing it from the edge of the book spine, so the marble can roll freely from the ramp. Measure the distance the marble rolls.
8. Explain to the students that this is the process they are to use in the experiment. Discuss the importance of controlling all variables (keeping everything the same except for the height of the ramp).

VIII. Procedure
1. Distribute the necessary materials.
2. Have the students work in small groups and set up the experiment.
3. Each group should have the student worksheets.
4. Each group should have one person to roll the marble, one or two to mark where the marble stops. Each student records the measurement on his individual worksheet.
5. Students are to roll the marble five times each at heights of 2 cm, 4 cm, 8 cm, 16 cm, 32 cm. They must always maintain a base of 88 cm. The marble must be released each time at the edge of the book spine.
6. The students measure the distance the marble rolls each time it is released.
7. Students record the measurement in cm on the data table.
8. They then find the average for each height and record it on the data table.
9. Students then complete the graph.

IX. What the Students Will Do
1. Measure the distance the marbles roll.
2. Record measurements in Data Table.
3. Total and average the trials for each height.
4. Graph the average distances.

X. Discussion
1. Did the height of the slope increase the distance the marble rolled? Why? Why not? (Yes, the marble has more potential (stored) energy with greater height.)
2. If the slope keeps getting steeper, will the marble roll farther each time? Why? Why not? (Up to a point, yes. When the slope is completely vertical, the marble will not roll far because its energy is absorbed by the ground.)

XI. Extension
1. Use different sized marbles.
2. Use different spheres—golfballs, ball bearing, etc.
3. Use different surfaces—rug, cement, dirt, table top, etc.

Construct a ramp for the marble

← Meter sticks

5 cm of masking tape

Start the marble from the book's spine

Measure distance marble rolled and record

DISTANCE

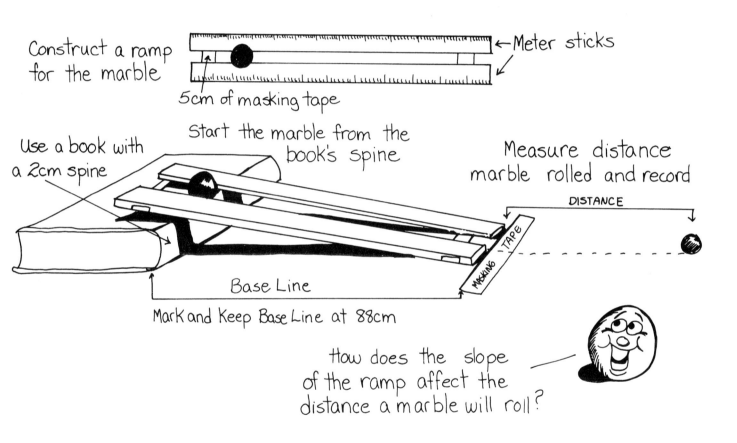

Use a book with a 2cm spine

Base Line

Mark and Keep Base Line at 88cm

How does the slope of the ramp affect the distance a marble will roll?

"It's Simply Marbleous"

Height	2 cm	4 cm	8 cm	16 cm	32 cm
Trial # 1					
Trial # 2					
Trial # 3					
Trial # 4					
Trial # 5					
Total					
Average					

DISTANCE MARBLE ROLLED IN CM

Construct a ramp for the marble

←Meter sticks

5cm of masking tape

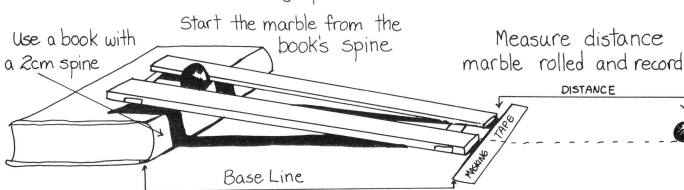

Use a book with a 2cm spine

Start the marble from the book's spine

Measure distance marble rolled and record

DISTANCE

Base Line

Mark and Keep Base Line at 88cm

How does the slope of the ramp affect the distance a marble will roll?

"It's Simply Marbleous"

Distance the
marble rolls
(cm)

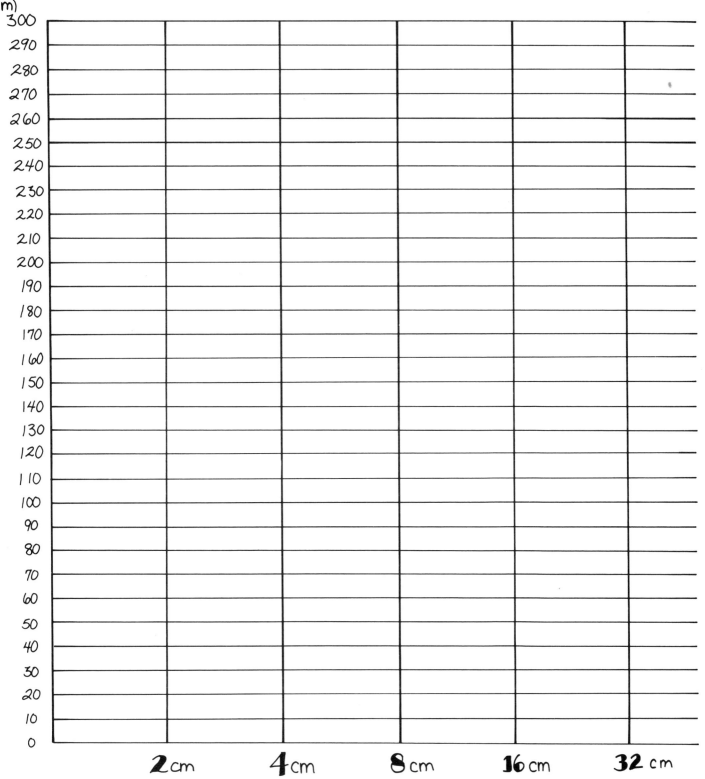

	300
	290
	280
	270
	260
	250
	240
	230
	220
	210
	200
	190
	180
	170
	160
	150
	140
	130
	120
	110
	100
	90
	80
	70
	60
	50
	40
	30
	20
	10
	0

2 cm   4 cm   8 cm   16 cm   32 cm

 # Count & Crunch

I. Topic Area
Gathering and Recording Data

II. Introductory Statement
In this investigation, students will determine the numerical frequency of the six colors of "M & M's"® plain candies. After the students have found the most frequent color of this popular candy, they will be rewarded by being allowed to eat `em up!

III. Math Skills
a. Whole Numbers
b. Percents
c. Fractions
d. Decimals

Science Processes
a. Observing
b. Classifying
c. Predicting/Estimating
d. Recording Data
e. Interpreting Data

IV. Materials (per group)
One small package of "m&m's"® candies
Pencil and crayons
Student worksheet

V. Key Question
What is the most frequent color of candies?

VI. Background Information
1. To find the percentage of each color, divide the number of each color by the total number of candies in the bag and multiply by 100.

Example:

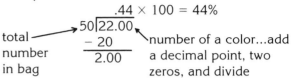

2. To find the ratio (fractional part) of each color, use the total number as the denominator and the number of each color as the numerator.

Example:

Number of a color ⟶ $\frac{22}{50} = \frac{11}{25}$ ⟵ reduced
total number in bag ⟶

3. Cost per candy is determined by dividing the cost by the total number of candies.

Example:

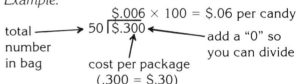

4. Sample data table with figures:

	Total No. of candies	No. of Green	Ratio	% of Gr.	No. of Orange	Ratio	% of Or.	No. of Yellow	Ratio	% of Yel.
Prediction	40	4	$\frac{4}{40}$	10	12	$\frac{12}{40}$	14	30	2	$\frac{2}{40}$	5
Actual	50	4	$\frac{4}{50}$	8	8	$\frac{8}{50}$	16	10	$\frac{10}{50}$	20

VII. Management Suggestions
1. Estimated time: one or two 45 minute periods.
2. Groups of two or more are recommended.
3. Students should record their own data.
4. Express ratios according to the appropriate ability level of your students.
5. Students should be aware before you begin that the candies are not to be eaten until the investigation is completeed.
6. Pocket calculators are great for computational work.

"m&m's" is a registered trademark of Mars Incorporated

MATH + SCIENCE: A SOLUTION   55   © 1987 AIMS Education Foundation

VIII. Procedure

1. Before opening the package, have students predict and record the total number of candies, the colors present, and the number of each color.
2. Open the package. Observe and sort according to color.
3. Record data in the table provided.
4. Calculate fractional or percentage parts of the total.
5. Graph the actual percentage of each color.

IX. What the Students Will Do

1. Predict color and content of the bag of candy.
2. Count and record actual numbers, ratios and percents in the data table.
3. Design a bar graph.

X. Discussion

1. What was the most common color? Least common?
2. Why do you think there are more browns than other colors?
3. Why do you think "m&m's" ® Brand Candies have been so popular over the years?
4. Why are there no blues?
5. Is there a difference in the taste from one color to another?
6. How would you set up an experiment to find out if the different colors taste different?

XI. Extensions

1. Do this investigation using "m&m's" ® Brand Peanut Candies as a comparison.
2. This investigation may also be done with other candies that come in assorted colors, i.e., Life Savers ® , gum balls, etc.
3. Have students construct bar graphs where each color is represented using crayons, colored pencils, or felt pens. The graph could demonstrate frequency of occurrence in any one of three math operations mentioned here.
4. If you have metric balances, have students weigh the candies in their packages. Compare with the weight listed on the package.
5. Have the students determine the cost per candy.
6. Make a class chart or bar graph showing the results of the entire class. You may wish to include class averages on this chart.
7. The more capable students could change the ratios to decimals, then percentages.
8. Another investigation for more capable students is "m&m's" ® "What's in the Bag".

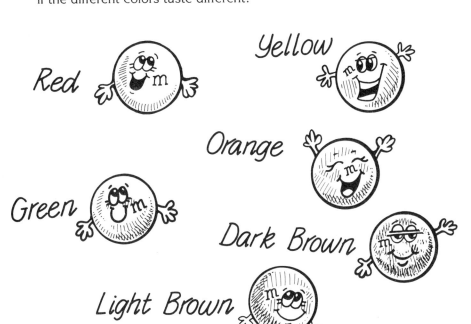

Red   Yellow   Orange   Green   Dark Brown   Light Brown

MATH + SCIENCE: A SOLUTION

m&m CHOCOLATE CANDIES m&M's CANDIES
Count & Crunch

Name: _____

	Prediction	Actual
1.		
2.		
3.		
4.		
5.		
6.		
7.		
8.		
9.		

1. How many M&M's are in your package?....
2. What is the most common color?.....
3. What is the least common color?....
4. What is the class favorite color?....
5. What is your favorite color?....
6. How much does your package weigh?....
7. How much does 1 M&M weigh?....
8. How much does your package cost?....
9. How much does 1 M&M cost?....

Fill in the Prediction part of the Data Table below. Next.....open your package and count the number of candies. Fill in the Actual part of both tables.

M&M Data Table

	Total # of M&M's	GREEN			ORANGE			YELLOW			LT. BROWN			DK. BROWN			RED		
		#	Ratio	%	#	Ratio	%	#	Ratio	%	#	Ratio	%	#	Ratio	%	#	Ratio	%
Prediction																			
Actual																			

Design a graph to display your results.

 # What's in the Bag?

I. Topic Area
Gathering and Recording Data

II. Introductory Statement
We will explore samples of bags of candies and attempt to determine if there are consistent patterns of manufacturing and packaging.

III. Math Skills
a. Adding
b. Dividing
c. Averaging
d. Graphing
e. Tabulating
f. Percent

Science Processes
a. Recording Data
b. Collecting Data
c. Identifying and Controlling the Variables
d. Hypothesizing
e. Interpreting and Predicting

IV. Materials (per group)
One bag of "m&m's" ® candies per group of three students
Colored pencils or crayons
Hand-held calculator (optional)
Student worksheets

V. Key Question
Does the "m&m's" ® / Mars Company package according to a systematic plan?

VI. Background Information
Sampling is a technique that makes it possible to make predictions that reflect a larger group picture. In other words,"You don't have to eat the whole ox to know the meat is tough." By looking at sample bags of candies, students can predict anticipated outcomes. The larger the sample, the more accurate the results.

VII. Management Suggestions
1. Three people are to work with one package of candies; one to count, one to record, and one to compute; all can work on computation and graphing.
2. Estimated time: two to three 45 minute periods.
3. Encourage students to show results of their investigation in a variety of ways: narratives, line graphs, pictographs, circle graphs, demonstrations.

VIII. Procedure
1. Take as many samples as possible up to eight. Each bag represents a sample.
2. Record the total number of candies as the number(N) for the mean and/or percentages.
3. Graph each of your samples by color.
4. By observation, establish the average number of each color. Then, compare this with the arithmetic mean.
5. Gather data from several groups in the class.
6. Determine percentage for each color in each sample and for all samples as a whole.
7. Design a graph to show the percentage of each color for each of your samples.
8. Discuss the Key Question and record your conclusions.
9. Propose questions that need further investigation.

IX. What the Students Will Do
1. Students will predict the number of candies in their sample. Keep the Key Question in mind at all times.
2. Students will look for central tendencies throughout this whole experience. They will compute the percentage of each color in each sample, and the mean of each color for all samples.
3. Predict what the total number of candies might be from their sample data.

X. Discussion
1. Does the "m&m's"/Mars Company package their product according to a plan? How does this data support or refute this idea?
2. What other products have similar packaging plans that might warrant further experimentation?

XI. Extensions
1. Other products such as canned foods— apricots, pears, peaches, etc.—can be sampled and predictions made about the quality and quantity of the product.
2. Letters could be sent to various companies regarding production control. Students may want to send a letter to the "m&m's"/Mars Company, Division of Mars, Inc., Hackettstown, New Jersy, 07840 to check on the production ratios of "m&m's" ® Brand Candies... if there are any.

"m&m's" is a registered trademark of Mars Incorporated

What's in the Bag?

m&m's® CANDIES

Grand Total

$$\% = \frac{\text{Color Number}}{\text{Total for Sample}} \times 100$$

Name: _____

	Total for Each Color	Average for Each Color

M&M® COLORS	Sample 1		Sample 2		Sample 3		Sample 4		Sample 5		Sample 6		Sample 7		Sample 8	
	No.	%	No.	%	No.	%	No.	%	No.	%	No.	%	No.	%	No.	%
Green																
Orange																
Yellow																
Light Brown																
Dark Brown																
Red																
Total for each Sample																

1. What is the average number of M&M's® in a bag? _____

2. Based on your samples, what can you say about the colors in a bag of M&M's®? _____

3. Show your results by graphing.

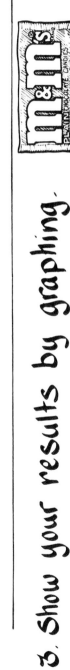

"m&m's" is a registered trademark of Mars Incorporated.

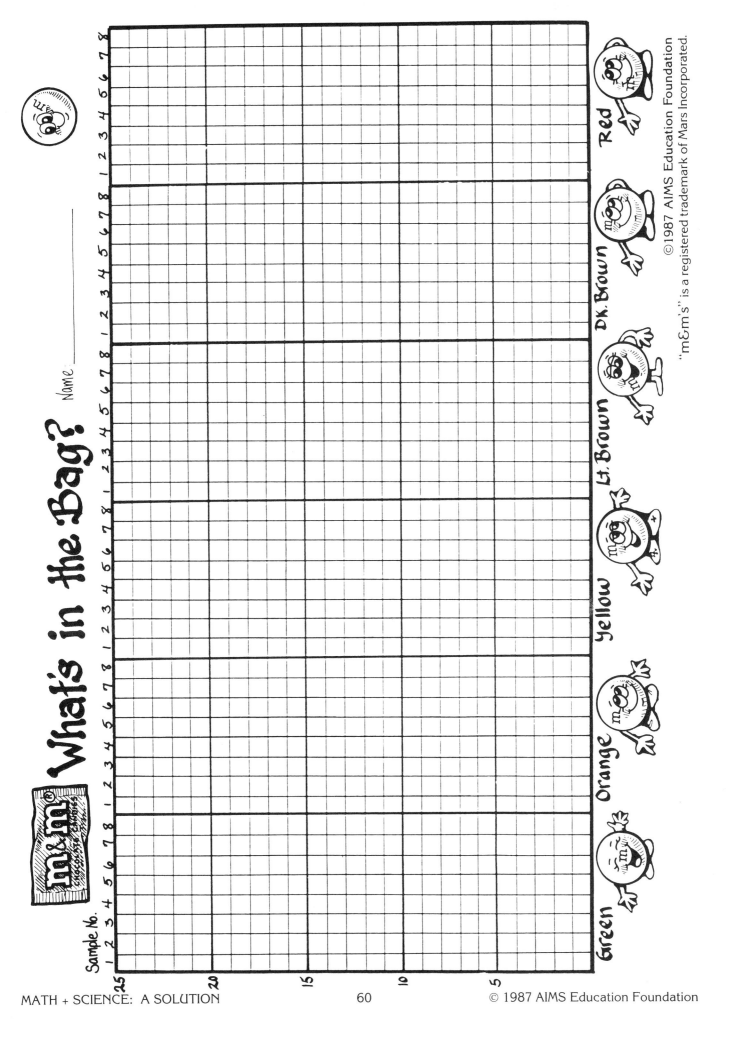

What's in the Bag?

Name _____

Sample No.

25
20
15
10
5

Green Orange Yellow Lt. Brown Dk. Brown Red

60

DEALING with DATA

I. Topic Area
Gathering and Recording Data

II. Introductory Statement
Students are often called upon to record data in tables and to read data from them. Unfortunately, too infrequently are they given the hands-on opportunity to ponder the problems of data table design, let alone actually design one.

By providing students with such experiences we make it easier for them to understand the logical meaning and natural organization of the data they are called upon to record and read!

In this investigation of inherited traits the students will gain skill in the design and use of a simple data table. They will also gain skill in the use of ratio in a simple problem solving situation.

III. Math Skills
a. Counting
b. Ratio
c. Estimating
d. Sampling

Science Processes
a. Observing
b. Predicting
c. Gathering and Recording Data
d. Interpreting Data

IV. Materials (per student)
Paper
Pencil
Ruler
Student Worksheet

V. Key Question
"What part of the school's population has the traits that you have?"

VI. Background Information
1. The trait pairs under study are "either/or" pairs.
2. The trait pairs under study are inherited.
3. In the key question we have written "WHAT PART OF THE SCHOOL'S POPULATION...," leaving it up to you, the classroom teacher, to pick the appropriate form in which the students are to express ratio (whole number, common fraction, decimal fraction, or percent).
4. Tongue rolling, widow's peak, and chin cleft are fairly common traits; ear wiggling is a rare trait.

VII. Management Suggestions
1. Students are to work in pairs.
2. One forty-five minute period is sufficient time for the data gathering and organizing. Often, the data interpretation and prediction revisions can be completed within the same period.
3. The typical student will require as much time to design and complete Data Table #4 as he/she requires to accomplish all previous tasks in the lesson.
4. Data for the whole class can be collected by student tally at the chalkboard or by show of hands as each trait is announced by the teacher.
5. The teacher will need to tell the students the size of the school's population.

VIII. Procedure
1. Ask the key question.
2. Provide materials.
3. Provide the correct figure for the school's population and direct students to complete Worksheet #1.
4. Provide a means by which the class data can be collected and summarized.
5. Direct the students to complete the Table of Class Data on Worksheet #2.
   NOTE: Traits must be filled in by students.
6. Ask the students to compare the class data with their original predictions; then direct the students to revise their predictions, construct a new data table in the space provided on Worksheet #2, and enter the revised predictions.

IX. What the Students Will Do
1. Each student will learn which trait of each pair he/she has and will check the appropriate boxes in Data Table #1.
2. Students will use their own data to help make a prediction about what part of the school's population has each of their own traits.
3. Students will complete the Class Data Table.
4. Students will compare class data to their predictions for the whole school and decide whether or not to make any revisions.
5. Whether or not the students choose to make revisions, they all should design and construct a new data table in the space provided.

6. Students will participate in the discussion and in the extension activity, if any.

X. **Discussion**

1. What kinds of problems do you think people have when they are asked to design and use a data table?
2. In our investigation we used tables with four columns, each having two rows. Why do you suppose the designer of these tables used that design?
3. What are some other ways we could have organized our data?

XI. **Extension**

1. This investigation can be extended to include other traits. Students would be asked to design appropriate data tables.
2. Students could be asked to predict how many class members have 2, 3, and all 4 traits in common. They would then be directed to construct appropriate data tables in which predictions and actual counts could be recorded.
3. Traits showing continuous variation, such as height, could be investigated. Students would be asked to wrestle with the problem of fitting highly variable data into an appropriate table. This could provide an excellent transition to graphing.

DEALING WITH DATA

WHAT PART OF THIS SCHOOL'S POPULATION HAS THE SAME TRAITS THAT YOU HAVE?

FIRST, PLEASE CHECK ☑ EACH TRAIT THAT YOU HAVE.

TRAIT PAIR #1		TRAIT PAIR #2		TRAIT PAIR #3		TRAIT PAIR #4	
EAR WIGGLER	☐	TONGUE ROLLER	☐	WIDOW'S PEAK	☐	CHIN CLEFT	☐
EAR NON WIGGLER	☐	TONGUE NON ROLLER	☐	NO WIDOW'S PEAK	☐	NO CHIN CLEFT	☐

NEXT, PLEASE ESTIMATE THE PART OF OUR SCHOOL'S POPULATION WHICH HAS EACH OF YOUR TRAITS. WRITE YOUR ESTIMATE IN THE TABLE BELOW.

THERE ARE _____ STUDENTS IN OUR SCHOOL.

TABLE OF ESTIMATES FOR TOTAL SCHOOL POPULATION

TRAIT PAIR #1	TRAIT PAIR #2	TRAIT PAIR #3	TRAIT PAIR #4
EAR WIGGLER _____	TONGUE ROLLER _____	WIDOW'S PEAK _____	CHIN CLEFT _____
EAR NON WIGGLER _____	TONGUE NON ROLLER _____	NO WIDOW'S PEAK _____	NO CHIN CLEFT _____

DEALING with DATA

LET'S FIND OUT WHAT PART OF OUR CLASS HAS EACH OF THE EIGHT TRAITS! PLEASE COMPLETE THE DATA TABLE BELOW AND PUT OUR CLASS DATA THERE.

TABLE OF CLASS DATA

NOW THAT YOU HAVE SEEN THE DATA FROM OUR CLASS, YOU MAY WISH TO REVISE SOME OF YOUR ESTIMATES FOR THE TOTAL SCHOOL POPULATION. TO DO THIS, PLEASE DESIGN YOUR OWN DATA TABLE AND MAKE YOUR REVISED ESTIMATES IN YOUR DATA TABLE.

SOME OF YOUR CLASSMATES ARE SURE TO HAVE REVISED THEIR ESTIMATES. WHAT KIND OF INFORMATION MIGHT HAVE LED THEM TO REVISE THEIR ESTIMATES?

_____

_____

_____

_____

Practically Pi

I. Topic Area
Interpreting Data

II. Introductory Statement
Children will understand that "pi" is a constant relationship between the circumference and the diameter of any given circle.

III. Math Skills
a. Measuring
b. Graphing
c. Decimal computation

Science Processes
a. Organizing Data
b. Interpreting Data

IV. Materials (per group)
Assorted circular containers
1 lb. coffee can
2 lb. coffee can
Soup can
Juice can
Wheel
Waste basket
Metal bookends
Meter stick or tape
Chalk or marker
String
Student Worksheet

V. Key Question
"How does the circumference of any circle compare with its diameter?"

"Brent found that the distance around a circle was a little over 3 times the distance through the circle. Do you think it makes a difference what size circle he measured? Let's find out."

VII. Management Suggestions
1. For greatest degree of accuracy, measure to the nearest millimeter.
2. Review correct reading and writing of decimal numbers to the tenths place.
3. Estimated time: one 45 minute class period.

VIII. Procedure
1. Measure the diameter of each circular object (the longest distance from edge to edge).
   One way to measure diameter:

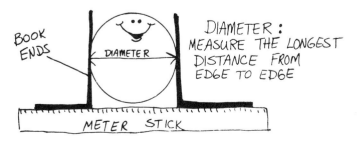

BOOK ENDS

DIAMETER: MEASURE THE LONGEST DISTANCE FROM EDGE TO EDGE

METER STICK

2. Record the diameter of each object in appropriate table on Student Worksheet.
3. Measure the circumference of each circular object. The circumference is the distance around the circle.

   One way to measure circumference is:
   a. Wrap a tape measure or string around the cylinder near the base. Then measure the string or tape.

METER STICK

   b. *Or* you may roll the cylinder one complete revolution along a meter stick or meter tape.

4. Record the circumference for each object in the table on the Student Worksheet.
5. Complete the Table:
   Column C—Express each ratio as a fraction or decimal ratio.

   Example: $\dfrac{C}{D}$ or C:D

   Column D—Divide each circumference by its diameter and record the answer in Column D.

IX. What the Students Will Do
1. Measure and record the circumference and diameter of various objects according to the above procedure.
2. Record the relationship of circumference to diameter and compute the decimal equivalents.
3. Discover the "constancy" of the relationship of circumference to diameter.

X. **Discussion**

1. *Observe:* What did you notice about the relationship between circumference and diameter in Column D? If you know the circumference of a circle, can you find the diameter? How? Can you find the circumference if you know the diameter? how?

2. What if you put the diameters and the circumferences measured into a graph? What would it look like? Use centimeter graph paper and try it!

XI. **Extension**

1. Introduce 3 unknown cylinders: A, B, and C. Give the diameters of A and B and the circumference of C. Can you find the missing figures?

2. Organize and record your data into a table. You may wish to draw a picture or cartoon also.

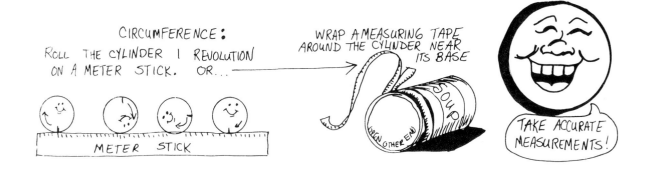

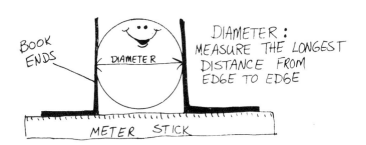

Practically Pi

How does the circumference of any circle compare with its diameter?

Cylinder	Diameter	Circumference	Ratio = $\dfrac{\text{Circumference}}{\text{Diameter}}$	Decimal Circumference ÷ Diameter
1 lb. Coffee Can				
2 lb. Coffee Can				
Juice Can				
Soup Can				
Wheel				
Waste Basket				

Take accurate measurements!

Circumference: Wrap a measuring tape around the cylinder near its base

Circumference: Roll the cylinder 1 revolution on a meter stick. or ....

Meter stick

Diameter: Measure the longest distance from edge to edge

Diameter

Meter stick

Book Ends

Just Drop It!

I. Topic Area
Interpreting Data

II. Introductory Statement
In this investigation, students will compare the amount of bounce that results from dropping different types of balls from various heights. The bounce resulting from dropping the balls on different surfaces can also be compared. From the collected data, a formula relating the height of bounce to the height of the drop will be developed. Using these formulas, students will be able to accurately predict how high a ball will bounce from any given height.

III. Math Skills
a. Formulating Equations
b. Graphing
c. Averaging

Science Processes
a. Interpreting Data
b. Applying and Generalizing

IV. Materials (per group)
One meter stick
At least two different types of balls to bounce
Student Worksheet

V. Key Question
"How is the bounce of a ball related to the height from which the ball is dropped?"

VI. Background Information
1. The data collected by dropping balls from an assortment of heights should result in a formula that shows the bounce to be proportional to the height of the drop.

Bounce = unknown factor times height of the drop

or

$$B = xh$$

Solving for x, $$\boxed{x = \frac{B}{h}}$$

2. A typical formula might be, $B = .55h$

The unknown factor (.55) is obtained by dividing the height of drop (h) into the height of the bounce (B).

3. Each different type of ball will have a different unknown factor, but this value will always be between 0 and 1.

4. *Sample Outcomes:*

Since .55 is most frequent, the formula would be $B = .55$ h (You may choose to average .72, .45, .59, .54, .59, .55, .55, .55, .54, .59 to determine your unknown factor, instead of simply picking the most frequently occurring number).

The formula $B = .55$ h means that for the type of ball used, the ball will bounce approximately 55% of the height from which it is dropped (.55 = 55%).

Height of drop (cm)	10	20	30	40	50	60	70	80	90	100
Height of Bounce (cm) (average)	7.2	9.0	17.6	21.6	29.6	33.0	38.3	44.3	48.6	59.6
Bounce ÷ Height	.72	.45	.59	.55	.59	.55	.55	.55	.54	.59

5. The data from the lower drop heights (10 cm, 20 cm, and 30 cm) will be the most inaccurate. Therefore, you may choose to omit this data when determining the formula for Bounce.

6. SUGGESTED BALLS: Tennis, Baseball, Ping Pong, Golf, Superball, Marbles. Each student group can do a different type of ball, or each group can test two or more different balls—teacher preference.

7. All bouncing heights and dropping heights are measured from the BOTTOM of the ball.

VII. Management Suggestions

1. ESTIMATED TIME: Three to four 45 minute periods.

2. Student groups of 3 or 4 work well. One can hold the meter stick, one can drop the ball, one can observe the bounce, and one can record the data.

3. To observe the bounce more accurately, the student should hold a piece of paper or cardboard at eye level in front of the meter stick. When the ball bounces, move the paper to the highest point the BOTTOM of the ball reaches. By sighting over the paper, the student can more easily read the measurement on the meter stick. A "hands and knees" observing position is a must—the observer must be at eye level with the ball at its highest point of bounce.

4. Hand calculators are greatly advised.

5. It is advisable to have all students use a hard floor or cement as their bouncing surface initially. Student groups that finish the investigation first can then be challenged to compare their results when a different surface is used.

6. It probably will be best to start your measurements with the 100 cm distance, and work down to the 10 cm distance. The lower height of drop distances are difficult to observe and measure.

7. If possible, you may wish to *start* all groups using the same type of ball in order to compare student data and measurement technique.

VIII. Procedure

1. Select the balls to be dropped.

2. Stand the meter stick vertically with the zero end down on the floor.

3. Place the bottom of the ball at the 10 cm mark of the meter stick. After releasing it, observe and record the total bounce in cm (distance from the floor to the highest point the bottom of the ball reaches at the peak of its bounce).

4. Repeat twice more for a total of three trials for each dropping height.

5. Repeat this same procedure for each of the remaining 9 dropping heights.

6. Record all data in the student sheet data table.

7. Plot the average height of bounce for each of the 10 dropping heights and construct a line graph.

IX. What the Students Will Do

1. Drop a ball 3 times for each of 10 dropping heights.

2. Record the height of the bounce for each trial on the data table.

3. Calculate the average height of bounce for each of the 10 dropping heights.

4. Construct a line graph of the data.

5. Write a formula relating B (height of bounce) to h (height of drop).

X. Discussion

1. Did any of the balls bounce as high or higher than the point from which it was dropped? (NO. A BALL WILL NEVER BOUNCE BACK UP TO THE POINT FROM WHICH IT WAS RELEASED).

2. What are some reasons that might explain why a ball can not bounce back up to the point from which it was released? (BECAUSE OF SUCH FACTORS AS AIR FRICTION, AND THE ABSORPTION OF ENERGY BY THE FLOOR, THE BALL LOSES ENERGY, AND THEREFORE CANNOT RETURN TO ITS PREVIOUS HEIGHT.)

3. The Bounce ÷ Drop Height numbers show what portion of the starting height (drop height) the ball is able to bounce up to. For any one ball, would you expect each of these numbers to be about the same, or different? (EACH TYPE OF BALL WILL BOUNCE A FIXED PORTION OF OF ITS STARTING HEIGHT. THAT PORTION IS THE UNKNOWN FACTOR. THE PURPOSE OF THIS INVESTIGATION IS TO EXPERIMENTALLY DETERMINE THIS UNKNOWN FACTOR. FOR ANY ONE BALL, THE BOUNCE ÷ DROP HEIGHT SHOULD BE ABOUT THE SAME. HOWEVER, THE LOWEST DROPPING HEIGHTS ARE DIFFICULT TO ACCURATELY MEASURE. THEREFORE, THESE COULD SHOW GREAT VARIATION. DIFFERENT TYPES OF BALLS SHOULD SHOW DIFFERENT BOUNCE ÷ DROP HEIGHT VALUES.)

4. If a certain ball has a bounce equal to .5 of the dropping height, predict the height of its bounce if dropped from a height of 10 feet. (BY USING THE FORMULA, B = xh, STUDENTS SHOULD BE ABLE TO SUBSTITUTE IN ANY GIVEN VALUE OF X TO DETERMINE OR PREDICT BOUNCE. IF h = 10 and x = .5 THEN .5 times 10 EQUALS *5 feet*.

XI. Extension

1. Inflate basketball with different amounts of air pressure. Find the relationship of air pressure to height of bounce.

Just Drop It!

Professor: _____

Scientist

Select a ball and surface to which it will be dropped. Let it fall the distances shown 3 times from each height. Measure the highest point of each bounce and find the average.

#1

Type of ball:	Type of surface:

Falling Distance in Centimeters		20	40	60	80	100
Height of Bounce in Centimeters	Trial #1					
	Trial #2					
	Trial #3					
	Sum					
	Average					

Write a formula relating B to h.
B = height of bounce
h = height of drop

B =   h

#2

Type of ball:	Type of surface:

Falling Distance in Centimeters		20	40	60	80	100
Height of Bounce in Centimeters	Trial #1					
	Trial #2					
	Trial #3					
	Sum					
	Average					

Write a formula relating B to h.
B = height of bounce
h = height of drop

B =   h

SCREEN TEST

I. **Topic Area:**
Searching for a representation of a million.

II. **Introductory Statement:**
Students will find how large a fiberglass insect screen needs to be in order to have approximately one million openings.

III. **Math Skills**
Estimating
Measuring to the nearest millimeter
Computing areas
Converting millimeters to centimeters
Converting square centimeters to square meters
Finding averages
Using information from a table

Science Processes
Observing
Estimating
Recording data
Interpreting data
Generalizing results

IV. **Materials:**
3 pieces of insect screen for each group
Metric rulers marked in millimeters
Screen Test worksheets
Meter sticks

V. **Key Question:**
How much is a million? Can we see a million of something?

VI. **Background Information**
How many of us have an idea of what a million of something looks like? In this investigation, students will have extensive experience in finding areas as they search for a million openings in the insect screen. Thorough instruction in finding areas should precede the investigation. As they convert from square centimeters to square meters it is important to know that there are $100 \times 100 = 10,000$ square centimeters in a square meter. It takes about 2.4 square meters of insect screen to have a million openings or holes.

VII. **Procedure**
The fiberglass insect screen is available at little cost from building supply stores. A roll that measures over 12 square feet costs about $3.00. Only about one square foot is needed to supply the required number of pieces. The screen is easy to cut with a scissor and leaves no sharp protruding ends as would metal screen. When cutting the screen, follow vertical and horizontal threads with care. Most screens have holes that are not square. Therefore, to obtain fairly uniform results, the sample screens should be cut to be approximately, but not precisely, square - approximately 3 to 5 centimeters square. Each group should receive three pieces of differing dimensions.

Introductory Activities:
1. Project the image of a section of screen about 3×5 cm on the screen using an overhead projector. Leave the image on for about five seconds.
2. Announce that you want each team to determine their best strategy for estimating the number of openings. Tell them that you will project the screen for about thirty seconds during which time they can execute their strategy. Give the teams several minutes to determine their strategy before flashing the image on the screen.
3. Record the estimates of each team. Then have someone check the number of openings and report it to the class. Let each team compute their per cent of error by dividing the amount of difference between their estimate and the count by the actual count.

Next have students follow the steps as outlined on the worksheets. The following hints might be helpful.
a. By placing the screen into a corner, the work is simplified.
b. Millimeters are changed to centimeters by moving the decimal one place to the left.
c. The easy way to find the number of openings is to multiply the number in each row by the number of columns.
d. To find the number of openings per square centimeter divide the number of openings by the number of square centimeters.
e. To find the number of square meters of screen needed divide the number of square centimeters of screen by 10,000.
f. To find the average length per opening divide the number of openings in a row by the length of the row measured in centimeters. Similarly, find the average width per opening.

IX. **Discussion**
1. Why did the results differ?
2. What effect would it have on the count of openings per square centimeters if the shape of the screen would have been 8 cm long and 2 cm wide? (The difference allowed for each opening per unit of length and width is different so it would give different results depending on how the piece was cut from the original screen.)

X. **Extension**
Students might suggest other ways of finding a million. For example, if the school yard is surrounded by a link fence, they could find how many openings there are between posts and from that determine how many "post" lengths would have one million holes. Such a daily presence as that of the fence would be remembered a long time after such a calculation. This extension also finds application for the area formula.

TEST

what does a million look like?

1. Place 3 samples from a roll of screen into the spaces on this page. Carefully mark the location of each of the corners.

2. Remove the screens and connect consecutive corners of each screen with line segments to form rectangles.

3. Measure the length and width of each screen to the nearest millimeter but record the measurement in centimeters correct to the nearest tenth. (68mm = 6.8 cm)

4. Make the required computations to complete the chart on the following page.

I look like a million today!

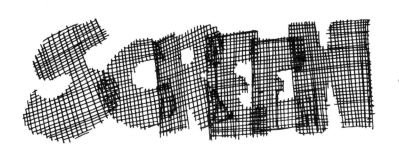

Average Number of Openings per Square Centimeter

Sample	Measurements in cm		Area in cm²	# of Openings per		Total # of Openings	Number of Openings per cm²
	Length	Width		Row	Column		

Total		
Average		

1. How many square centimeters of screen would it take to contain a million openings?

2. How many square meters of screen would it take to contain a million openings?

   Use one sample only for the following:

3. What is the average length *per* opening in the screen?

4. What is the average width *per* opening in the screen?

Trial & Error Learning

I. Topic Area
Interpreting Data

II. Introductory Statement
The student will discover that data from an investigation can be used to construct a model (graph) which can, in turn, be interpreted to provide information about real world events.

III. Math Skills
a. Telling and Recording Time
b. Time Computation
c. Minute to Second Conversion
d. Generalizing from Graphs

Science Processes
a. Gathering and Organizing Data
b. Interpreting Data (Graphs)

IV. Materials
Student Worksheets
Clock with second hand
Construction paper 12″ × 18″ (30 cm × 45 cm)
"Scotch" type tape

V. Key Question
"How do you learn by trial and error?"

VI. Background Information
The maze can be stapled to a sheet of 12″ × 18″ construction paper for portability. A second sheet of construction paper with a 5/8″ diameter hole in the center should cover the maze *at all times.*

VII. Management Suggestions
1. Each student is to work independently.
2. This activity requires one full 45 minute period on the first day, plus 15-25 minutes on each of the next two days.
3. The student will need to be reminded of the importance for timing each trial and for resisting the urge to mark on or peek at the maze.
4. For students who "forget" and peek, a different, but equivalent maze can be made easily by tracing the mirror image of the regular maze (turn the maze page over and trace).
5. Timing of each trial begins when the student first starts through the maze and ends only when the END is found or when 5 minutes of wandering has not been rewarded by finding the END.
6. The teacher should do this investigation beforehand in order to be prepared for unanticipated problems.

VIII. Procedure
1. Ask the key question.
2. Gently guide discussion to arrive at class consensus as to the precise meaning of the problem at hand.
3. Set up the mazes with construction paper covering the maze and the hole in the construction paper aligned with "START."

4. Provide necessary instruction concerning recording of starting and finishing times.
5. Point out that it is common for students to take more than 5 minutes to complete the maze during the first few trials.
6. Inform students that any times greater than 5 minutes should be recorded as 300 + seconds due to graph scale limit...or encourage students to design their own graph scales to accommodate times greater than 300 seconds.
7. Provide materials (worksheets, clock).

IX. What the Student Will Do
1. Each day for three consecutive days, or on each of three days spaced equally, the student will negotiate the maze 5 times.
2. The student will keep track of time taken for each trial by recording all starting and ending times in the data tables.
3. The student will graph each day's trials on the same graph, using pencil of different color for each day's trials. (The result will be three graph lines on the same graph paper).
4. The student will use his/her graph to find evidence of learning, forgetting, and maze mastery.

X. Discussion
Before Activity
1. KEY QUESTION—HOW DO YOU LEARN BY TRIAL AND ERROR?
2. Why does a mouse maze or rat maze seem so simple when viewed through human eyes? (Is it intelligence or just perspective?)
3. How would you set up a maze for humans so that you could have a fair contest between humans and rats?
4. Would it be important in a "trial and error learning" situation to keep the subject from seeing the whole maze at once?

After Activity
5. What evidence do you have that learning took place during the 5 trials of any given day?
6. What evidence do you have that learning took place from day to day?
7. What evidence do you have that "forgetting" took place from day to day?
8. How can you tell (from your graph) when you have really mastered the maze?

XI. Extension
1. Construct new mazes with fewer or more choices and attempt to correlate learning to difficulty of the maze.
2. Allow student to leave a trail (pencil line) on the maze. Then determine by what factor the times improve. Discuss whether or not this would be considered "trial and error learning."
3. After all discussion, assign a written story requiring the student to write about all interpretations he/she could make from the graph.

Trial & Error Learning

_____ NAME

PLEASE PUT DOWN YOUR "TIME TAKEN" IN TOTAL SECONDS.

DAY 1

TRIAL NUMBER	TIME STARTED	TIME FINISHED	TIME TAKEN (SECONDS)
1			
2			
3			
4			
5			

TABLE 1

PLEASE FINISH MAKING THE DATA TABLE.

DAY 2

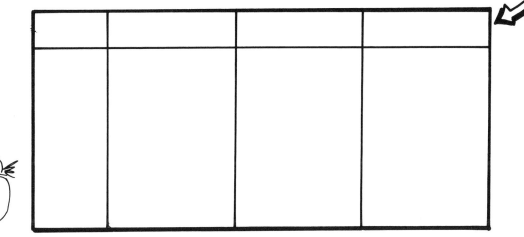

TABLE 2

PLEASE DESIGN YOUR OWN DATA TABLE!

DAY 3

TABLE 3

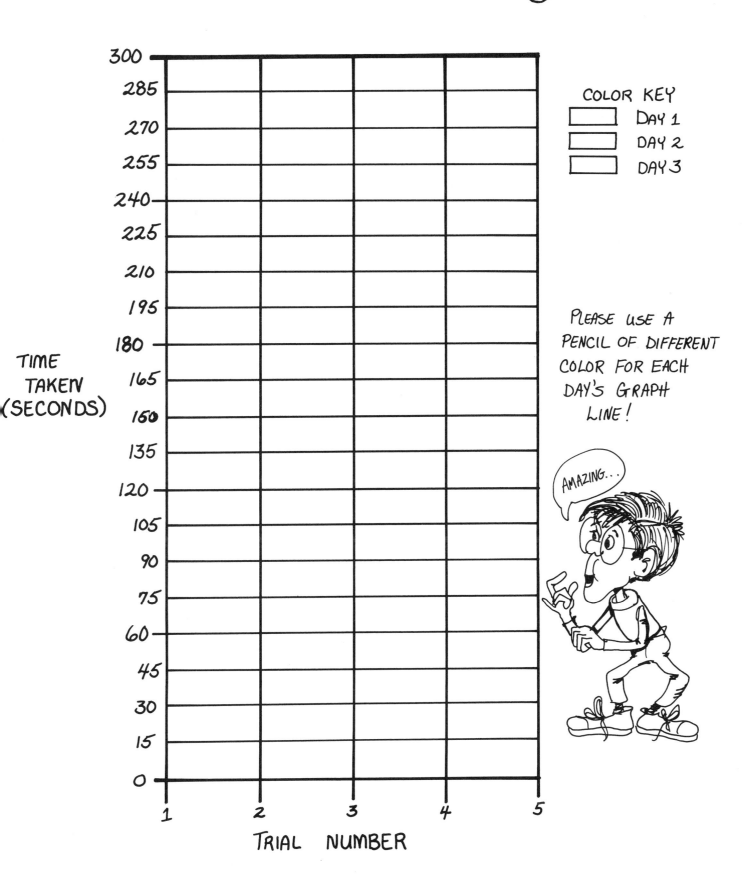

Trial & Error Learning

_____ NAME

COLOR KEY
☐ DAY 1
☐ DAY 2
☐ DAY 3

PLEASE USE A
PENCIL OF DIFFERENT
COLOR FOR EACH
DAY'S GRAPH
LINE!

AMAZING...

TIME TAKEN (SECONDS)

300
285
270
255
240
225
210
195
180
165
150
135
120
105
90
75
60
45
30
15
0

1   2   3   4   5

TRIAL NUMBER

Trial & Error Learning

NAME

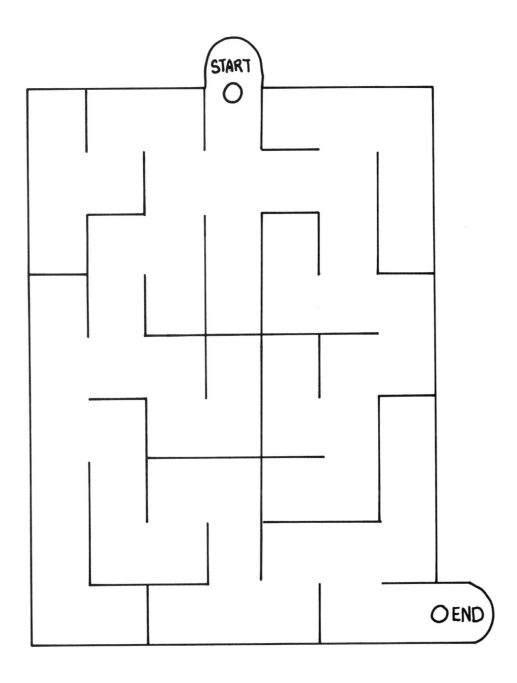

START

END

Trial & Error Learning

PLEASE WRITE A STORY WHICH TELLS WHAT YOUR GRAPH LINES SHOW ABOUT TRIAL & ERROR LEARNING.

_____

_____

_____

_____

_____

_____

_____

_____

_____

_____

_____

_____

_____

_____

_____

_____

_____

_____

_____

_____

_____

Graph = Feet-EE

I. Topic Area
Graphing Skills, Metric Measurement

II. Introductory Statement
In this beginning graphing activity, students will trace their foot on a piece of construction paper, measure the overall length of their foot "cut-out" in centimeters, and will help to construct a bar graph using the cut-outs of all the students in class. The activity provides a good opportunity for the teacher to discuss the parts of a graph, and beginning graphing concepts.

III. Math Skills
a. Graphing
b. Metric Measurement

Science Processes
a. Interpreting Data
b. Measurement
c. Predicting

IV. Materials
Construction Paper
Scissors
Metric Rulers
Masking Tape
Index Cards
Student Worksheet

V. Key Question
"What foot length is the most common in our class?"

VI. Background Information
1. A GRAPH is a diagram that shows numerical relationships.
2. A graph always has four main parts: a TITLE, an ORIGIN, a VERTICAL AXIS, and a HORIZONTAL AXIS.

3. Notice that each axis is labeled and marked off in a number scale.
4. In numbering the axes on a graph, two rules must be followed. First, the numbers assigned to an axis must change equally from one line to the next (example: 2, 4, 6, 8, on the vertical axis all increase by two). And second, the range of numbers on an axis must be large enough to include the largest value you have to represent on that axis (example: If a student's foot is larger than 25 cm, the horizontal axis in the above graph would have to be extended). Note: All numbers are placed on lines, not between lines!

VII. Management Suggestions
1. This activity requires a large, clear wall approximately 6 feet by 6 feet on which to construct a graph. Outside building walls work very well. It is possible, however, to do this inside on a wall or chalkboard.
2. If taking students outside, it would be best to have the wall prepared beforehand with a vertical and horizontal axis. You can use masking tape to do this:

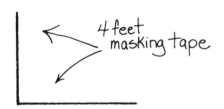

4 feet masking tape

Title:
Number of Students
Of Each Foot Length
In Our Class

Note: Notice that the numbers are written on lines, not between lines.

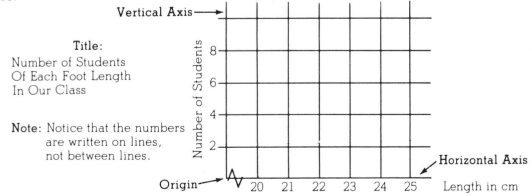

3. The day before you do this activity, you may want to warn students to wear clean socks on the following day, as they will have to take off their shoes to trace their feet.

4. TIME ESTIMATE: One 45 minute class period.

VIII. Procedure

1. In the classroom, have students remove a shoe and trace their foot on a piece of construction paper. You may wish to give boys and girls a different color paper so that a visual comparison between boys' feet and girls' feet can be made.

2. Next, students are to cut out this foot print, predict its overall length to the nearest centimeter, and then measure accurately.

3. This length must be written somewhere near the center of the footprint.

4. The students then take their footprints to a wall that the teacher has previously prepared with a masking tape graph.

5. A brief discussion of the main components of a graph, and basic graphing concepts should be initiated by the teacher.

6. Then, the teacher should ask the key question: WHAT FOOT LENGTH IS MOST COMMON IN OUR CLASS? Perhaps a graph can help to answer this question.

7. The teacher then asks: "Who feels that their foot is the smallest?" The smallest footprint can then be taped to the graph in the position below:

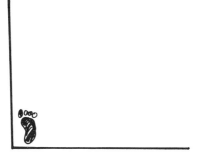

If more than one student has this length footprint, the footprints are taped in a vertical line like this:

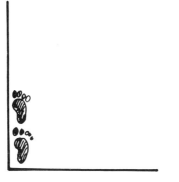

8. Larger sizes are then taped next to the smaller ones. Be sure that if a certain length is not represented in your class, a space is left on the horizontal axis such that the numbering always increases by the same amount:

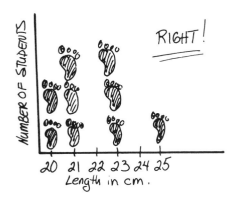

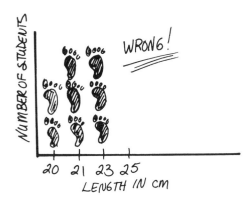

9. Continue until all footprints have been taped to the wall. Then tape index cards to the wall that label each axis. One should read "Number of Students"; the other should read "Length in cm." Likewise, cards should be used to label the numbers on each axis.

10. Review the discussion questions, and then have students reproduce the wall graph on graphing paper.

IX. **What the Students Will Do**

1. Trace their footprint on construction paper, and predict its length in centimeters.
2. Measure the footprint to the nearest centimeter.
3. Place their footprint in the appropriate place on the wall graph (with teacher assistance).
4. Reproduce the class wall graph on graphing paper.

X. **Discussion**

1. What does the vertical axis (on the wall) represent? (NUMBER OF STUDENTS)
2. What does the horizontal axis represent? (LENGTH OF THE FOOTPRINT IN CM)
3. Which footprint length is the most common? (AN-SWER FOUND BY LOOKING AT THE GRAPH).
4. Which footprint length is the least common? (AN-SWER FOUND BY LOOKING AT THE GRAPH).
5. Can you make any generalizations, or do you notice any trends on this graph? (USUALLY, THERE ARE ABOUT AS MANY VERY SMALL SIZES AS VERY LARGE SIZES, ALSO MOST FOOTPRINTS WILL BE FOUND SOMEWHERE IN THE MIDDLE OF THE GRAPH, FEW ARE AT THE EXTREME ENDS.)
6. Try to discuss with students the concept that graphs make data easier to analyze. It is easy to see which foot length is most common because it will have the tallest bar on the graph.

XI. **Extension**

1. Fill a large mouth gallon jar (or even a large plastic bag) with 3 different colors of dried beans (red, white, and pink). Have students use a spoon or fork to pick up as many beans as they can. Then line the beans up by color, and construct a BEAN GRAPH.

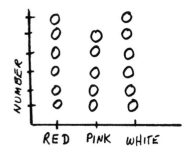

2. If available, use CENTICUBES (centimeter cubes) and centimeter graphing paper, and do the same activity above using the cubes instead of the beans.
3. Make similar graphs of students' heights.
4. Try to correlate foot size and height.
5. Put this activity on a bulletin board display. Let students write graffiti on the cut out feet!
6. To convert the Bar Graph to a Line Graph, connect a piece of yarn to the feet:

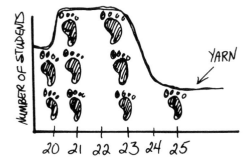

Graph = Feet-EE

———————name

Predict the length of your foot in centimeters:

Prediction _____ cm

Now, measure: Actual _____ cm

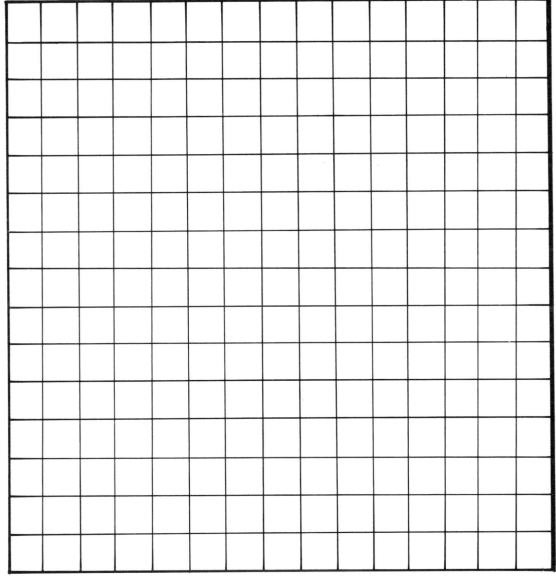

Number of 👣

Length of 👣 in cm

MATH + SCIENCE: A SOLUTION   82   © 1987 AIMS Education Foundation

The Penny Sort & Nickel Dates
By Arthur Wiebe

Topic Area
Statistics, economics

Introductory Statement
Students will classify pennies and nickels by minting dates; determine medians and modes; construct real, representational, and abstract bar graphs; and interpret results.

Math	Science
Classifying	Predicting
Constructing real, representational, and abstract bar graphs	Observing
	Classifying
	Collecting and organizing data
Completing tables of information	Comparing and analyzing
Determining medians and modes	Reporting data
	Interpreting data
	Drawing conclusions

Materials
For each group:
   1 roll of pennies, current circulation
   1 roll of nickels, current circulation
   Colored markers for graphs
   Optional: hand lens

Key Question
   What can we find out about the age of pennies and nickels that are in current circulation?

Background Information
   Although some statistical analyses involve data on all of the people or objects studied, most analyses make use of a random sample which is assumed to be representative of the total population from which it is taken. Random samples are used when studying every single unit would be costly, inconvenient, or even impossible. The key to all statistical surveys used to define the nature of any population from a sample (of anything, not just people) is random selection. If samples are truly random, they will simulate what is known as a chance distribution and will allow the study to produce data that are unbiased and summaries that are valid.
   In this investigation, randomness is achieved by selecting rolls of coins that are known to have been in recent circulation, as opposed to coins that may have been accumulated during a specific time period or according to some selective criterion. Using rolled coins will also ensure that no one connected with the investigation has even had opportunity to look at the coins beforehand. The concept of randomness should be stressed to students since it is fundamental.
   The fact page *A Penny's Worth of Thoughts* provides additional background information. The median minting date of pennies in circulation is about three years previous to the current year. This means that one-half of all of the pennies in circulation have been minted during the last three years! The median minting date of nickels is significantly earlier but still not as long ago as most would predict without this experience.
   Bar graphs, otherwise known as histograms, are a way to display data. They may be constructed vertically or horizontally, and the bars must all be the same width. Bar graphs are used for data which are noncontinuous: that is, for data that are distinct from one another. An example of continuous data would be plant growth over a period of time; although growth might be recorded on two adjacent days, it would be reasonable to assume that the growth was continuous. On the other hand, an example of noncontinuous data would be the number of boys and girls in a certain classroom; the two categories are distinct.
   There are several kinds of bar graphs. In this investigation, three types are used: real, representational, and abstract. A real bar graph contains rows or columns of spaces, each large enough to contain a single object. Usually real graphs are used on the floor, although theoretically there is no reason why objects could not be glued to the graph and then the graph hung on a wall or bulletin board. Representational bar graphs are similar to real graphs, except that they can be a different size with pictures or symbols. Abstract bar graphs have the rows or columns shaded or colored to display the information desired.

Management Suggestions
1. Currently circulating coins are available at banks and the school cafeteria. Because of the whole-class activities with combined data built into

this investigation, it is necessary to use different coins for all groups; reusing coins will result in duplicate graphs and invalid conclusions.

2. NOTE: Beforehand, the real graphs *Penny Sort* and *Nickel Dates* must be extended to accommodate the assortment of minting dates usually included in a roll of coins. To do this, make a second copy of each page, cut off the heading by cutting across the tops of the columns, and then paste it onto the first copy below the corresponding columns.

3. This activity is designed to be used by cooperative learning groups with five students, each identified with letters A, B, C, etc; and with roles assigned as follows:

   • Student #1 is responsible for receiving and returning coins (see Step 4 below).
   • Student #2 is responsible for recording all responses as well as data on the tables.
   • Student #3 is responsible for the construction of the real graphs.
   • Student #4 is responsible for constructing the representational graphs.
   • Student #5 is responsible for gathering the representational graphs from the other groups and constructing the abstract bar graphs.

4. One way to ensure that all coins are returned is to treat it as a problem-solving assignment before the investigation. Challenge students to arrange a roll of coins in a perfect array or some other arrangement easily counted. For example, 50 pennies could be arranged in a 5x10 array or 5 stacks of 10 pennies. Students could help decide which method is best.

5. If more than four groups are formed, additional copies of the two summary pages (Pages 3 and 6) must be provided for each group.

Procedure

The Penny Sort (Pages 1, 2, and 3)

1. Discuss the *Key Question*: "What can we find out about the age and other characteristics of pennies and nickels that are in current circulation?"

2. Organize the cooperative learning groups and assign roles. Agree upon the method to be used in checking the number of coins.

3. Distribute pennies to Student #1, who counts them and reports any discrepancy.

4. Using *The Penny Sort* (Page 1) and Student #2 as recorder, each group makes predictions.

5. Using the real bar graph (Page 2), Student #3 writes the present year in the blank farthest to the right. Then the preceding years are filled in

in reverse order to the left, *with the first two years the same.*

6. All students in each group work together to classify the coins by their minting dates. Student #3 builds the real graph, starting at the bottom of each column.

7. Student #2 records the actual results beside the predictions on Page 2 and then fills in the table at the bottom of the page.

8. Student #4 makes the real graph into a representational graph by coloring the penny in each space that contained a coin. Student #1 counts and returns the pennies.

9. Using Page 3, Student #5 uses the representational graph to make a bar graph. Groups circulate their representational graphs to other groups so that this same student can copy them.

10. As a class, compare the predictions with the actual results using Page 3. Identify and discuss the types of bar graphs: real, representational, and abstract. .

Nickel Dates (Pages 4, 5, and 6)

Repeat the investigation described above, except that nickels are substituted for pennies.

Aging Pennies and Nickels (Pages 7, 8, 9, and 10)

1. Explain that now the groups will compare the minting dates of pennies and nickels of the whole class.

2. Using *Aging Pennies* (Page 7), Student #2 records data from Page 2 on the table. Complete the page, discussing the terms *median* and *mode* as appropriate.

3. Using *Aging Nickels* (Page 8), groups do the same with data on nickels.

4. Using *Aging Pennies and Nickels* (Page 9), Student #4 builds a abstract bar graph. Help students to judge how to use part of a space. Ask the individual groups to analyze the data and record their observations.

5. Provide opportunity for the groups to share their observations and conclusions with the whole class.

6. Distribute the fact sheet entitled *A Penny's Worth of Thoughts* (Page 10) and discuss the information.

Discussion

1. How many pennies (nickels) are in a roll?

2. Explain the difference among the different types of bar graphs: real, representational, and abstract.

3. (Page 7) What are the median minting dates of pennies examined by each individual group? How do they compare with the median of the

composite or total date?

4 What effect does the size of the sample seem to have on the median minting date?

5. Which median minting date is likely to be closest to that of the 30,000,000,000 pennies in circulation? [the median of the largest sample] Repeat this discussion with respect to nickels.

6. How do you explain the difference between the median minting dates of pennies and nickels?

7. Why do so many pennies disappear from circulation?

Extensions

1. Ask students to list all the things they see on the two sides of the pennies and nickels:
   Whose profile is on the front?
   What building is pictured on the back?
   What expressions are found on both pennies and nickels?
   What other information is shown?

2. Find out the range of minting dates (the earliest year subtracted from the most recent) for both pennies or nickels examined by the class.

Curriculum Correlations

Language arts/social studies: Have students do research and write reports on any of the following:
   The people shown on any of our coins
   The history of the U.S. Mint
   Counterfeiting
   Currency of other countries, including quotations of current value in U.S. dollars in daily newspaper.

Music: Find and learn some school or popular songs about coins or currency, such as *Pennies From Heaven*. State any standards for acceptability beforehand!

Home Link

Repeat the investigation using quarters. Beforehand, ask students to predict median and mode of minting dates. Ask students to gather the relevant data from quarters in the possession of their parents without bringing the coins to school. This could be done over a period of several days, making sure no coins are tabulated twice.

The Penny Sort

Classify by their minting dates the 50 pennies from a roll of pennies that has been in circulation recently. You may need a hand lens to be able to read the date on some pennies.

Before you begin, make your best guess in response to the following:

	Guess	Actual

1. How many pennies do you think will have been minted in this year? _____ _____

2. How many pennies do you think were minted in the last full year? _____ _____

3. In which year do you think the oldest penny was minted? _____ _____

4. Out of this set, which year will have the most pennies represented? _____ _____

5. When these pennies are arranged in order of minting dates, in which year do you think the middle two pennies (Nos. 25 and 26) were minted? _____ _____

Now classify the pennies and enter the information in this table. Compare your guesses with the actual result. Then build a real graph using the pennies on the graphing sheet.

Minting Year	Before								
Number of Pennies									

The Penny Sort

Treasury Agents

year

Before

The Penny Sort

Construct a bar graph for each sample.

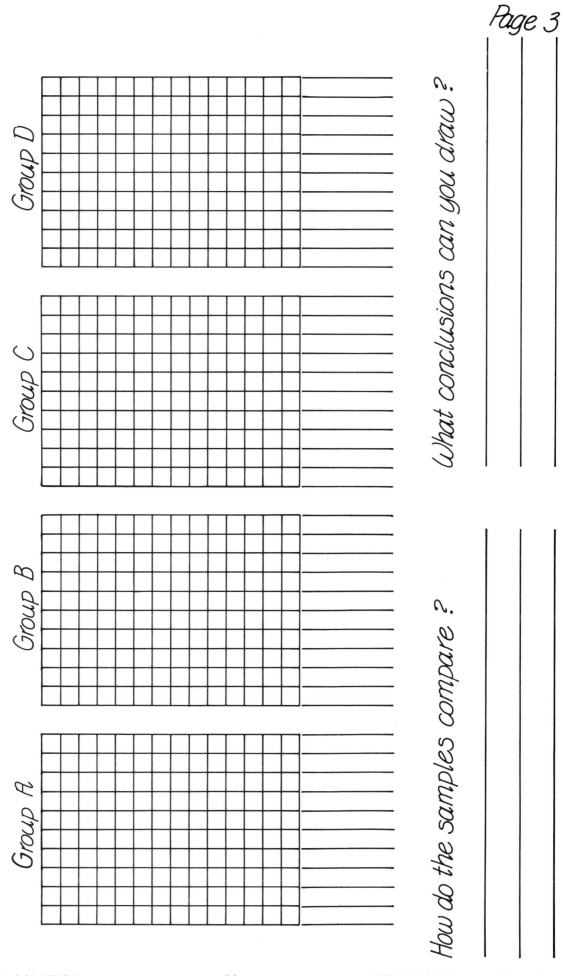

Group A

Group B

Group C

Group D

How do the samples compare?

What conclusions can you draw?

Nickel Dates

Classify by minting dates the 40 nickels from a roll of nickels that has been in recent circulation. Use a hand lens, if necessary, to read the date of minting.

Before you begin, make your best guesses in response to these questions.

	Guess	Actual

1. How many of these nickels were minted this year ?   _____ _____

2. In which year was the oldest nickel minted ?   _____ _____

3. When the nickels are arranged in minting date order, in which year were the middle two (Nos. 20 and 21) minted ?   _____ _____

4. In which year were most of the nickels in this roll minted ?   _____ _____

If you have done the Penny Sort investigation, how do you think the minting date distribution of nickels will compare with those of pennies?

_____

_____

Why ? _____

_____

_____

Minting Year	Before									
Number of Nickels										

Nickel Dates

Examining Team

year

Before

Nickel Dates

Construct a bar graph for each of the samples.

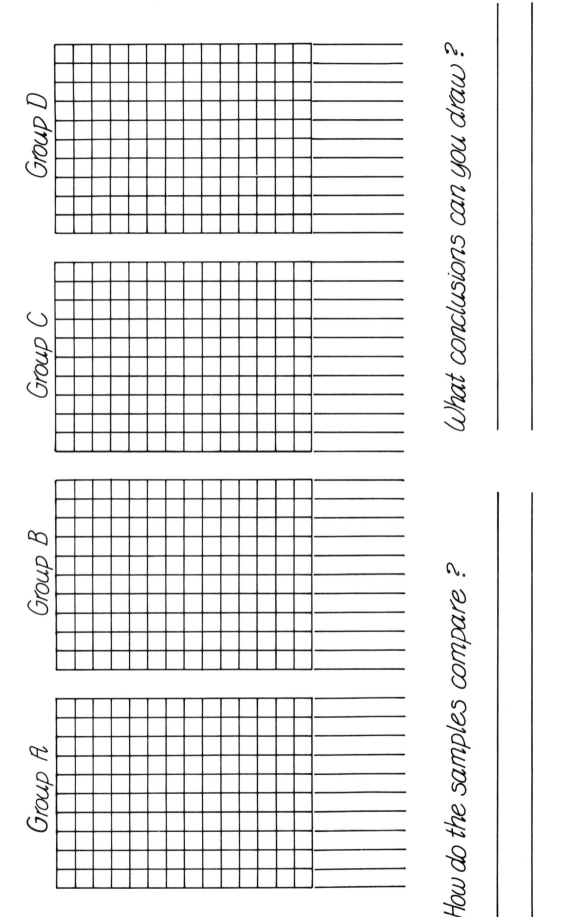

Group A

Group B

Group C

Group D

How do the samples compare?

What conclusions can you draw?

Aging Pennies

How do minting dates of pennies and nickels compare?

Collect the information from each group and record it in this table. Counting from either end, in which year were the two middle pennies minted?_____ This is the **median** minting year for pennies. Color the block for each group's median.

Minting Dates of Pennies

	Years Minted									
	Before									
A										
B										
C										
D										
E										
F										
G										
H										
Totals										

Groups

Now find the total number minted in each year. Determine the **median** and **mode** of this larger sample. Mark or color the spaces in which these are found. How old is the median penny?

_____years

Aging Nickels

How do minting dates of pennies and nickels compare?

Collect the information from each group and record it in this table. Counting from either end, in which year were the two middle nickels minted?_____ This is the **median** minting year for nickels. Color the block for each group's median.

Minting Dates of Nickels

	Years Minted								
	Before								
A									
B									
C									
D									
E									
F									
G									
H									

Groups

Totals									

Now find the total number minted in each year. Determine the **median** and **mode** of this larger sample. Mark or color the spaces in which these are found. How old is the median nickel?

_____years

Aging Pennies and Nickels

How do minting dates of pennies and nickels compare?

Please construct a bar graph to compare the number of **pennies** the class examined that were minted in any one year with the number of **nickels** minted in that same year.

Minting Dates of Pennies and Nickels

Before	*pennies*											
	nickels											
	pennies											
	nickels											
	pennies											
	nickels											
	pennies											
	nickels											
	pennies											
	nickels											
	pennies											
	nickels											
	pennies											
	nickels											
	pennies											
	nickels											
	pennies											
	nickels											
	pennies											
	nickels											

Years in Which Coins Were Minted

0   5   10   15   20   25   30   35   40   45   50   55

Number of Coins

We observed that _____

_____

_____

_____

_____

A Penny's Worth of Thoughts

In the United States, as in most other countries, only the government may mint or manufacture money.

The nation's first mint opened in Philadelphia in 1792 when that was the nation's capital.

The mints make our coins. The Bureau of Printing and Engraving and the Federal Reserve make our paper money. Most of the coins in general circulation are minted in Denver and Philadelphia. Coins for collectors and investors are made in San Francisco and West Point, New York.

Each year the U.S. Mint produces 14 billion (14,000,000,000) pennies. This is 78 percent of all U.S. coins. It is also 25 percent of all coins minted annually in the whole world.

Before 1982, most pennies were made of copper. Since then, they have been made of zinc with a very thin copper coating. Because zinc has less mass than copper, today's pennies are lighter. Nickels are made of a mixture of copper and nickel.

The cost of minting a penny is 0.6 of a cent. This means the government "makes" 40 cents for each 100 pennies minted. By comparison, it costs only 2 cents to make each $100 bill, leaving a "profit" of $99.98. It costs less than 3 cents to make a nickel or quarter, less than 2 cents to make a dime, and less than 6 cents to make a half-dollar.

In 1857 the American half-cent was abolished because of its low value. But in 1976, Congress refused to act to discontinue minting pennies. The reason given was that it would acknowledge that inflation has really taken place.

If we didn't have pennies, would we would understand the meaning of expressions such as "a penny saved is a penny earned" or "a penny for your thoughts"?

Every year, more than five billion pennies - $50,000,000 worth - disappear from general circulation. Where do they go?

The RubberBand STRETCH

I. Topic Area
Applying and Generalizing

II. Introductory Statement
In this investigation students will explore a cause and effect relationship with rubber bands and other common materials; specifically, they will add mass to the system illustrated on student page and measure the stretch of the rubber band for each mass added. After graphing their data, students will develop a formula relating stretch to mass added.

III. Math Skills
a. Measuring Length and Mass
b. Counting
c. Discovering Patterns
d. Developing a Formula
e. Applying a Formula

Science Processes
a. Measuring
b. Predicting and Estimating
c. Controlling Variables
d. Collecting and Recording Data
e. Interpreting Data
f. Applying and Generalizing

IV. Materials
Rubber bands 5-6 cm in diameter by 1 mm thick by 2 mm wide (or similar)
Paper cups
Large paper clips
Tape
Lots of pennies
Metric ruler
Student Worksheet

V. Key Question
"How much does a rubber band stretch?"

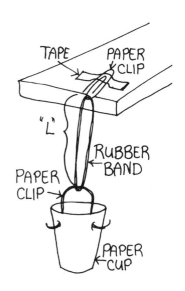

VI. Background Information
1. The data table and graph are set up for rubber bands of the characteristics described above.
2. Pennies are one of the least expensive kinds of masses to use in an investigation. 200 pennies will suffice for a class of 30 working in groups of 3. A few replacement pennies are recommended.
3. Pennies minted after 1981 have less mass than those minted during or before 1981. This is a very minor factor.
4. Several variables are at work in this investigation; most deal with age, size, composition, and general condition of the rubber bands, and with how many times and how much rubber bands have been stretched. Students should be allowed to discover these variables on their own.
5. At least two sources of error are possible: 1) pennies' masses vary, as pointed out above, and 2) students will not always make measurements from the same vantage point, thus causing up to ±1 mm error per measurement. By calling student attention to this and perhaps by demonstrating it, error can be reduced to ±0.5 mm per measurement... or, students can be left to discover this error on their own.
6. Mathematics convention is to put the dependent variable on the left side of the equation, i.e. $S = 1/3\,M$ where S is the dependent variable. When teaching a cause-effect relationship, however, it may add clarity if we ignore this convention and write $M = 3S$ instead of $S = 1/3M$.

VII. Management Suggestions
1. As a full-scale science investigation, two periods of 45 minutes each are required; as a math exercise, one period will suffice.
2. Each team has three roles: 1) ruler positioner, 2) measurement reader, and 3) mass adder/recorder.

VIII. Procedure

Day One - Investigating to Collect Data

1. Put together the materials.
2. Ask key question and allow students to state their ideas.
3. The need for focusing upon a "do-able" investigation will arise. Tell students what materials are available and focus discussion.
4. Provide materials.
5. Roam to aid teams in need of direction.
6. Students who finish early should be encouraged to graph their data and to suggest reasons why their graph lines are not perfectly straight.

Day Two - Interpreting Data, Generalizing, and Applying

1. Provide instruction on graphing, as needed. Those who have finished or will finish quickly should be encouraged to run the investigation again, trying to maintain better control over variables and trying to reduce measurement error.
2. Provide large group instruction on developing formulas.
3. Suggest an application problem as a contest. "Use your team's formula to predict how much the rubber band will stretch when we add 40 pennies."

IX. What the Students Will Do

Day One

1. Students will participate in discussion centered on key question.
2. Students will work in teams of three to collect and record data.

Day Two

1. Students will graph data.
2. Advanced students will give consideration to the shape of their graph lines.
3. Students will participate in large group activity in which a general formula is developed to relate S (amount of stretch) to M (mass added).
4. Students will use formula to make a prediction.

X. Discussion Questions

Before Gathering Data

1. HOW DOES A RUBBER BAND STRETCH?
2. What are the ways a rubber band can be stretched?
3. What do you think are the important factors influencing how a rubber band stretches?
4. (NOTE: Sketch the system on the blackboard). If we were to stretch a rubber band by adding mass (weight) to a system like the one on the blackboard, what information would we need to keep track of?

After Gathering Data

1. Please tell me what you know about formulas.
2. Provide information needed for development of a general formula from the student data.
3. "Use your team's formula to predict how much the rubber band will stretch when we add 40 pennies."

XI. Extension

1. Compare rubber bands of different characteristics.
2. Proceed to next investigation: RUBBER BAND SHOOT

MATH + SCIENCE: A SOLUTION

© 1987 AIMS Education Foundation

The RubberBand STRETCH

How Much Does A Rubber Band Stretch?

Please fasten a paper cup "pan" to one end of a rubber band with a large paper clip. Suspend the system from your table or desk top. It should resemble the drawing at the right.

Measure the length of the rubber band as it hangs there. Call its length "L".

L=____mm

Begin your investigation by adding ____ to the paper cup ____ at a time, and measure the length the rubber band stretches for each ____ added. Record the amount of stretch in the table.

TAPE   PAPER CLIP

"L"

RUBBER BAND

PAPER CLIP →

PAPER CUP

Total mass Added (g)													
Total Stretch (mm)													

NEXT, MAKE A LINE GRAPH WHICH SHOWS HOW MUCH THE RUBBER BAND STRETCHED AS MASS WAS ADDED TO THE CUP.

Amount Of Stretch in cm

inally, write a ormula relating S (amount of stretch) o M (mass added)

S = ____ M

50
45
40
35
30
25
20
15
10
5
0

5g 10g 15g 20g 25g 30g 35g 40g 45g 50g 55g 60g 65g
MASS ADDED

Rubber Band SHOOT!

I. Topic Area
Applying and Generalizing

II. Introductory Statement
This investigation can stand alone or it can be used as the second of two closely related investigations (see RUBBER BAND STRETCH in this booklet). In this investigation students will explore a cause and effect relationship with rubber bands; they will stretch the rubber band (cause) and measure how far it travels when released (effect). After graphing their data, students will develop a formula (using their data) which relates distance traveled to the amount of stretch.

III. Math Skills

a. Measuring Length and Mass
b. Counting
c. Discovering Patterns
d. Developing and Applying Formula

Science Processes
a. Measuring
b. Predicting
c. Controlling Variables
d. Gathering and Recording Data
e. Interpreting Data (Graphs)
f. Applying and Generalizing

IV. Materials
Rubber bands 5-6 cm in diameter by 1 mm thick by 2 mm wide (or similar)
Metric ruler
Meter stick or metric measuring tape
Student Worksheet

V. Key Question
"How does a rubber band shoot?"

VI. Background Information
The data table and graph are set up for rubber bands of the characteristics described above.

Several variables are at work in this investigation; most deal with the characteristics of the rubber band and with shooting techniques.

VII. Management Suggestions
1. This investigation may precede, follow, or replace RUBBER BAND STRETCH as a generalizing and applying exercise.
2. One full 45 minute period is required for this investigation.
3. Teacher should test a rubber band prior to class to see how much stretch results in the maximum safe distance traveled.

4. Class should be rearranged so that each team of two students has a clear firing range about 3 meters long.
5. Class should be informed of the maximum stretch allowed and the need to insure that rubber bands do not fly beyond the limits of the firing ranges.

VIII. Procedure
1. Begin class by playing with a rubber band.
2. Ask students the key question.
3. Accept ideas.
4. Provide materials.
5. Monitor for safety.
6. Provide instruction regarding developing a formula.

IX. What the Student Will Do
1. Students will participate in discussion centered on key question.
2. Students will work in teams of three to collect and record data.
3. To gather data student teams will stretch a rubber band by a measured amount, release it downrange, and measure the distance traveled.
4. Students will stay within the maximum safe stretch limit imposed by the teacher.
5. Students will graph data and verbalize the general relationship between stretch and distance.
6. Students will participate in a discussion which narrows the general relationship to symbols and numbers (from their own data).

X. Discussion Questions
Discussion before the activity should focus on achieving consensus as to the meaning of the key question, the design of the investigation, and the need to investigate safely.

Discussion after the activity may focus on relating this investigation to the RUBBER BAND STRETCH, or on dealing with the variables which were discovered during the investigation.

XI. Extension
1. Compare the behavior of rubber bands of different characteristics.
2. Devise a formula which combines the formula developed in this investigation with the formula developed in RUBBER BAND STRETCH, and then use the new formula to predict how far a rubber band would shoot if the equivalent of X g were applied to stretch the rubber band. This would provide a door through which students could enter the realm of weight, gravity, and forces in general.

Rubber Band SHOOT!

If You Stretch A Rubber Band, How Far Will it Fly?

First, measure the length of the rubber band with all the slack pulled out of it. Call its length "L".

L = _____ mm

Next, stretch your rubber band on a ruler by 10mm (L+10mm) and release it. Measure the distance it travelled in cm and record this distance in the data table. Repeat the process, each time stretching the rubber band by 10mm more. Complete the DATA Table.

Total Stretch (in mm)	10	20	30	40	50
Total Distance (in cm)					

Now, make a line graph of your data to show how far the rubber band travelled as you increased the stretch.

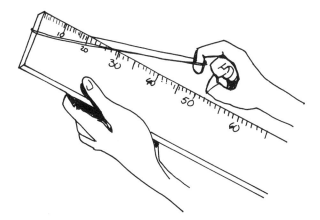

Finally, write a formula relating D (distance travelled) to S (amount of stretch).

D = _____ S

IT'S BEAN FUN!

I. Topic Area
Sampling

II. Introductory Statement
The concept of sampling and ratios will be explored in this investigation. By sampling jars full of 3 different colored beans, students will determine the color ratio of the beans in each jar.

III. Math Skills
a. Statistics/Probability
b. Ratio
c. Problem Solving
d. Logic
e. Averaging

Science Processes
a. Interpreting Data
b. Applying/Generalizing

IV. Materials (per class)
5 large mouth gallon jars (if unavailable, large plastic bags will work).
3 different colored dried beans (pink, red, and white), 4 lb. bag of each color
1/4 cup measuring cup
5 tablespoons
Student Worksheet

V. Key Question
"Can you determine the color ratio of the beans in each jar?"

VI. Background Information
1. *RATIO:* A comparison of two numbers by division. For example, the ratio of 4 to 6 can be written 4/6, 4 ÷ 6, 4:6, or 4 to 6.
2. *VOLUME:* The amount of space a material occupies, or takes up.
3. *COLOR RATIO:* Color ratio is the number of pink beans and red beans to white beans in the jar. It is found by taking several samples of equal volume and comparing the numbers of each color bean counted. Example:

Count

Sample	Red	Pink	White
1	10	12	2
2	5	11	4
3	9	15	1
4	12	12	1
Total	36	50	8

	Red	Pink	White
Therefore, the color ratio =	36 :	50 :	8
Divide each by 8 to get	4.5 :	6.2 :	1

Note that the white beans are the least in number. Therefore, we divide each ratio by the smallest number to calculate ratios to 1. Therefore there are 4.5 times as many red beans as white beans, and 6.2 times as many pink beans as white beans in this jar.

The color ratio is established by the teacher when each jar is initially filled.

4. *VOLUME RATIO:* The volume ratio is defined as the ratio of the volume of each of the beans in the jar. Because the beans are of different size, an equal number of each color bean will result in different volumes. The volume ratio is established by the teacher when the jars are initially filled.

5. When sampling the jars, each student must use a uniform sampling device. If using a tablespoon, *all* students must use the same kind and size spoon.

6. Make sure that before a student samples from a jar, all the beans taken out in a previous sample have been RETURNED TO THE JAR, and the sample has been stirred.

VII. Management Suggestions
1. Estimated time: two 45 minute class periods.
2. Try to use at least one bean that is much larger than the other two beans.
3. You may choose to set up fewer or more jars. Five is suggested if this is to be a total class activity. Student groups can then rotate through and sample each jar. This activity can work with only one jar, but other arrangements will have to be made for those students not actively sampling.
4. *TO FILL THE JARS:* Fill up a 1/4 cup measuring cup and count how many of each type of bean it takes to fill the 1/4 cup. (For accuracy, you may wish to take 3 samples of each color bean, and find an average number). Once you know how many beans it takes to fill the cup, simply count the number of cup-fulls of each bean that you put in the jar. Example:

	White Lima	Red Bean	Pink Bean
1/4 cup =	39	151	175

By putting 5 - ¼ cups of each color in a jar you will have:

$39 \times 5 = 195$ White Lima Beans
$151 \times 5 = 755$ Red Beans
$175 \times 5 = 875$ Pink Beans

Thus, your color ratio will be:	195	:	755	:	875 or
(Divide by 195)	1	:	3.8	:	4.5 or
Approximately	1	:	4	:	4

Because you used the same volume for each color bean (5-1/4 cups), the volume ratio is 1 : 1 : 1.

5. The other jars can be filled with different numbers of each color by varying the number of 1/4 cups used to fill the jar. This will change the color ratio and the volume ratio. Try these combinations:

Number of 1/4 Cups			Volume Ratio			Color Ratio		
White	Red	Pink	White	Red	Pink	White	Red	Pink
6	3	3	2 :	1 :	1			
2	4	2	1 :	2 :	1			
2	2	6	1 :	1 :	3			
1	6	3	1 :	6 :	3			
4	8	2	2 :	4 :	1			

6. Each jar that students sample should have different bean color ratios.

7. Averages and ratios *should not* be calculated by the student until all jars have been sampled. The teacher may choose to do these calculations as a large group activity.

8. After students have calculated their ratios for each jar, the teacher should place the true color ratios on the board without identifying which ratios belong to each jar. In this way, students can compare their results with the known values, and match their values to the known ones.

9. Student Worksheet, p. 103 has been provided in the event that beans other than white, pink, and red are used.

VIII. Procedure

1. Discuss the concept of color ratio with the students.

2. Place the jars around the room at different locations.

3. Divide the class into as many groups as you have jars. There should be no more than 6 students to a group. Each group will complete all the data for their jar and when finished will move to another jar. Students will continue sampling and recording data until all the data for all jars is completed.

4. Students will sample a jar as follows:
   a. Using a fork or spoon, the student will pick up as many beans as possible, and place them on the table.
   b. The beans will be separated by color, and each color will be counted and recorded in the data table under "SAMPLE 1".
   c. All beans will then be returned to the jar and a second sample will be taken, counted, and recorded under "SAMPLE 2".
   d. Finally, a third sample will be taken in the same way.
   e. Ratios and averages *should not* be done by students until all jars have been sampled.

5. When all sampling is completed, averages and ratios can be determined, and the Student Worksheet completed. Then, the student ratios can be compared to the known values.

IX. What the Students Will Do

1. Sample beans from jars by counting and recording the numbers of each color bean.

2. Find the average number of each color in a sample for each of the jars.

3. Calculate the color ratio of the beans in each of the jars.

X. Discussion

1. Besides the color ratio, what other ratios could be calculated by sampling the beans? (Volume ratio; Broken to Unbroken beans)

2. How could we measure the volume ratio of the beans in a jar? (Use a standard unit of volume, such as a small pill bottle. Take 2 or 3 large samples of the beans, and then fill the pill bottles with separate color beans. The number of full bottles of each color will represent the volume ratios; OR use a graduated cylinder to find the volume of each color taken from several samples).

3. What variables might have affected the outcome of the color ratio experiment? (Size of the beans; Steady hands of the samplers)

4. What real world ratios could be studied? (Ratio of unemployed to employed people; Ratio of number correct on a test to total number of problems; Ratio of cost to benefit; Ratio of increased wages to increased buying power; Ratio of hits to at bats)

XI. Extension

1. Try using jelly beans instead of dry beans. Test to see if using a uniform size (jelly bean) changes the accuracy of student results.

2. Try graphing the average number of each color bean in each jar. Do this on one piece of graph paper.

3. Estimate the total number of beans in one jar—closest to the correct number gets a prize! Have students sample the jar to determine the actual number.

4. Sample and calculate the volume ratios for the jars.

5. Try using a different sampling device (fork, measuring spoon, etc.)

6. Tell students the actual number of scoopfuls of beans in a jar. Have students predict and determine the total number of scoopfuls for each color bean.

7. Try converting ratios to percents.

8. Calculate the percentage error for estimates of total number of beans in the jar, and/or color ratios.

_____ NAME

JAR	BEAN or COLOR	SAMPLE 1	SAMPLE 2	SAMPLE 3	AVERAGE
A	WHITE				
	PINK				
	RED				
	COLOR RATIO OF BEANS ___ : ___ : ___ WHITE PINK RED				
B	WHITE				
	PINK				
	RED				
	COLOR RATIO OF BEANS ___ : ___ : ___ WHITE PINK RED				
C	WHITE				
	PINK				
	RED				
	COLOR RATIO OF BEANS ___ : ___ : ___ WHITE PINK RED				
D	WHITE				
	PINK				
	RED				
	COLOR RATIO OF BEANS ___ : ___ : ___ WHITE PINK RED				
E	WHITE				
	PINK				
	RED				
	COLOR RATIO OF BEANS ___ : ___ : ___ WHITE PINK RED				
F	WHITE				
	PINK				
	RED				
	COLOR RATIO OF BEANS ___ : ___ : ___ WHITE PINK RED				

_____ NAME

IT'S BEAN FUN!

JAR	BEAN OR COLOR	SAMPLE 1	SAMPLE 2	SAMPLE 3	AVERAGE
A					
	COLOR RATIO OF BEANS _____ : _____ : _____				
B					
	COLOR RATIO OF BEANS _____ : _____ : _____				
C					
	COLOR RATIO OF BEANS _____ : _____ : _____				
D					
	COLOR RATIO OF BEANS _____ : _____ : _____				
E					
	COLOR RATIO OF BEANS _____ : _____ : _____				
F					
	COLOR RATIO OF BEANS _____ : _____ : _____				

THE BIG BANANA PEEL!

What Part of a Banana is EDIBLE?

I. Topic Area
Estimating, measuring and generalizing.

II. Introductory Statement
In this investigation the students will determine what percentage of a banana is edible. By sampling several bananas, the students will develop a formula relating the edible part to the total mass of the banana.

III. Math Skills
a. Finding Mass
b. Using Ratios
c. Finding Percentages
d. Graphing
e. Writing a Formula
f. Averaging

Science Processes
a. Measuring
b. Recording Data
c. Interpreting Data
d. Generalizing

IV. Materials (per class)
A supply of bananas
Scales with masses
Student Worksheet

V. Key Question
"What part of a banana is edible?"

VI. Background Information
1. This may be the students' first experience in writing a formula. If so, the development of a formula needs to be discussed. In this case, the edible part of a banana (E in the formula) is to be expressed as a fraction or percentage of the total mass of the banana (T in the formula). Thus, if one-half of the banana is edible, the formula would be $E = 1/2T$. Most bananas will come very close to fitting the formula $E = .65T$ or $E = 2/3T$.

2. If desired, the average or the median percentage may be used. If either term is used, introduce the students to the term being employed.

VII. Management Suggestions
1. Before students begin, have them predict and record the edible percentage of a banana.
2. Students may work in groups of five with each member of each group having one banana and actually carrying out all of the activities. The members in a group would then pool their information.
3. Estimated time: one or two 45 minute periods.

IX. What the Students Will Do
1. Predict the percentage of a banana that is edible.
2. Measure the mass of the unpeeled and peeled banana and record the results.
3. Find the ratio of the edible part to the total mass.
4. Find the percentage that is edible.
5. Graph the percentage that is edible.
6. Graph the results of other members of the group.
7. Write the formula for the edible portion.

XI. Extension
This may lead to finding edible portions of other foods such as fruits, steaks, etc. The cost per kilogram or gram of the edible portion could be computed.

THE BIG BANANA PEEL!

USE **5** BANANAS TO
FIND THE ANSWER

What Part of a
Banana is EDIBLE?
_____ %

FIRST....
Complete the
Table.

	TOTAL MASS IN GRAMS	MASS OF PEELING (g)	MASS OF EDIBLE PART (g)	RATIO OF EDIBLE (g) / TOTAL MASS (g)	PERCENT OF BANANA THAT IS EDIBLE
BANANA A					
BANANA B					
BANANA C					
BANANA D					
BANANA E					
SUM					
AVERAGE					

NEXT.... CONSTRUCT A BAR GRAPH SHOWING THE PER CENT OF EACH BANANA THAT IS EDIBLE.

	0% 10% 20% 30% 40% 50% 60% 70% 80% 90% 100%
BANANA A	
BANANA B	
BANANA C	
BANANA D	
BANANA E	
AVERAGE	

FINALLY... WRITE A FORMULA TO SHOW THE AMOUNT OF THE EDIBLE PORTION. LET **E** STAND FOR EDIBLE AND **T** FOR THE TOTAL.

$$E = \quad T$$

GOING BANANAS

I. Topic Area:
Estimation and Measurement

II. Introductory Statement:
Students will make predictions and estimates relating to bananas and check them by testing and measuring.

III. Math Skills
a. Estimation
b. Measuring mass
c. Measuring length
d. Computing percentages
e. Cumputing percent of error

Science Processes
a. Estimation
b. Measuring mass and length
c. Predicting
d. Drawing conclusions
e. Formulating hypothesis

IV. Materials
Student worksheets
Scales and masses
Metric rulers or tapes
Bananas, one for each student group

V. Key Questions
a. Will the whole banana, the pulp, or the peeling of a banana float or sink?
b. What percent of the banana is edible as ordinarily understood?

VI. Background Information
In the age of hand-held calculators and computers, the skill of estimation is crucial. In this activity students will refine their concepts of metric lengths and masses by "guessing and testsing."

Bananas that are ripe will have a higher percentage of edible than those that are green. The size of the banana generally has little effect on the percent that is edible.

VII. Management
1. This activity, including the computation and excepting questions 7 and 8 will take about one class period of 40 minutes.
2. If questions 7 and 8 are to be tested at the same time, bananas at various stages of ripeness with other factors controlled should be available.
3. Students should first make individual predictions and guesses and then work in cooperative learning groups to discuss those predictions. A concensus need not result but the discussion should sharpen the focus on the estimation.
4. After students have tested their predictions and computed the percent of error, discussion on the process and refinement of guesses should be discussed.

VIII. Procedure
1. Students will make their individual predictions.
2. Students will discuss their predictions in small groups and may change their individual predictions.
3. Students will measure and test to obtain the experimental results.
4. Students will determine their percent of error by dividing the difference between the guess and the actual by the actual.
5. The class will discuss methods of refining such guesses.
6. The class will formulate hypothesis as in questions 7 and 8.

IX. Extensions
1. The percent of edible in various types of bananas and conditions of ripeness will be explored.
2. The percent of waste in other fruits will be examined.

Going Bananas

For each of the following, give your estimate or best judgment. Then, apply the test to the banana or bananas you are examining. Determine the per cent of error by dividing the difference by the actual.

	Prediction	Test Result

1. Will the whole banana sink or float? _____ _____

2. Will the pulp (peeled) of the banana sink or float? _____ _____

3. Will the peeling of the banana sink or float? _____ _____

4. What is the mass of the banana in grams?

Guess: _____ grams
Actual: _____ grams
Difference: _____ grams
Per Cent of Error _____ %

5. What is the length of the banana in centimeters?

Guess: _____ cm
Actual: _____ cm
Difference: _____ cm
Per Cent of Error: _____ %

6. Considering mass, what per cent of the banana is edible (pulp)?

EDIBLE?!

Guess: _____ %
Actual: _____ %
Difference: _____ %

7. Considering mass, does the ripeness of the banana make a difference? State your hypothesis and explain how you would test your hypothesis.

_____

_____

8. Considering mass, does the per cent that is edible change with the size of the banana? State your hypothesis, test it, and report the results.

_____

_____

The Truth About Bananas

Scientific Name

Family: Musaceae

Genus: Musa

Species: Musa acuminata (common banana)

Musa Paradisica (plantain banana)

OUR FAMILY

Food Value

Water : 75.7 %
Protein : 1.1 g.
Fat : 0.2 g.
Carbohydrates : 22.2 g.
Ash : 8 g.

Food Energy : 85 calories
Vitamin A : 190 IU
Thiamine (B_1) : 0.05 mg.
Riboflavin (B_2) : 0.06 mg.
Phosphorous : 26 mg.
Potassium : 370 mg.
Vitamin C : 10 mg.

Niacin : .7 mg.
Calcium : 8 mg.
Iron : .7 mg.
Sodium : 1 mg.

Is my percentage of water the same as yours? higher? lower?

Which of these statements are true?

a. The banana is a berry.

b. Bananas grow on trees.

c. Pound for pound, bananas are the most widely sold fruit in the United States.

d. Bananas are highly nutritious and easily digestible.

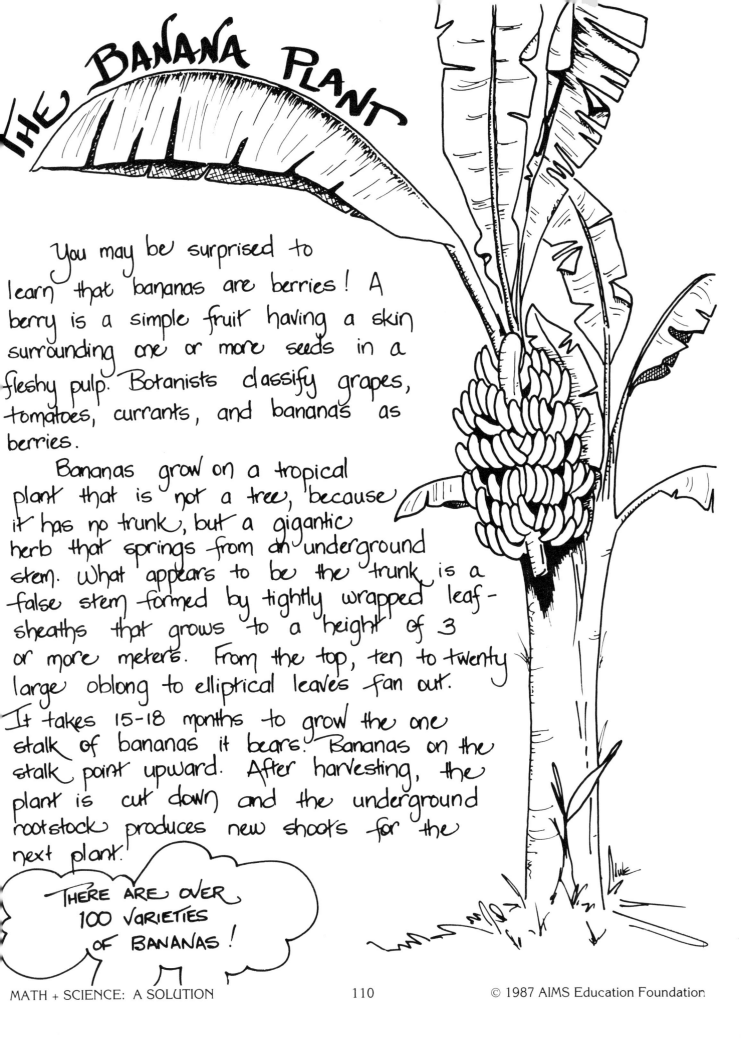

THE BANANA PLANT

You may be surprised to learn that bananas are berries! A berry is a simple fruit having a skin surrounding one or more seeds in a fleshy pulp. Botanists classify grapes, tomatoes, currants, and bananas as berries.

Bananas grow on a tropical plant that is not a tree, because it has no trunk, but a gigantic herb that springs from an underground stem. What appears to be the trunk is a false stem formed by tightly wrapped leaf-sheaths that grows to a height of 3 or more meters. From the top, ten to twenty large oblong to elliptical leaves fan out. It takes 15-18 months to grow the one stalk of bananas it bears. Bananas on the stalk point upward. After harvesting, the plant is cut down and the underground rootstock produces new shoots for the next plant.

THERE ARE OVER 100 VARIETIES OF BANANAS!

The Banana as Food

Pound for pound, bananas are the most widely sold fruit in the United States. They are the most important of all commercial fruits, close to the combined production of all citrus fruits.

Bananas are an excellent food source of potassium, vitamins A & C, and quick energy. They are low in protein and fat. They are an excellent between-meal snack and one of the most easily digested and nutritious natural foods. A medium size banana has about 125-130 calories, or about one calorie per gram.

Bananas come with their own wrapping, ready to go into lunch boxes. They are tasty sliced on breakfast cereals, in fruit salads, and gelatin desserts. An easy-to-make banana shake consists of one whole peeled banana and a cup of milk mixed to smoothness in a blender. A raw egg and a little nutmeg may be added for taste. Bananas are recommended for low-fat, low-sodium diets. The banana is at its best eating condition when the bright yellow peeling is flecked with brown specks, known as "sugar specks".

Plantains, a cooking variety of bananas larger than our common banana, is a staple food in the tropics. They are starchy when green. Plantains take the

place of potatoes. Plantain chips are the Latin-America equivalent of our potato chips!

Bananas are used in the preparation of flavorings. Vacuum dehydration yields banana crystals, a light-brown powder used in ice cream, bakery products and milk-based beverages.

"Tree-ripened" would not make good advertising for bananas. If allowed to ripen on the plant they are starchy, mealy, or rotten and therefore inedible. They arrive on the market dead green and are ripened in air-tight rooms with controlled humidity and temperature. These conditions permit nearly all of the starch to be converted into sugar for good taste. The best condition in which to buy bananas is when they are bright yellow with a green tip. Look for plump, well-filled fruit.

The HISTORY

of BANANAS

It is generally agreed that the banana originated in Malaysia and the East Indies. It is frequently referred to in ancient Hindu, Chinese, Greek, and Roman literature and in sacred texts of Oriental cultures. It is said that the armies of Alexander the Great fighting in India were the first Europeans to learn about bananas.

Theophratus, in a book written in the 4th century B.C. and considered to be the first scientific botanical work known, described the banana. The Arabs introduced them to the Near East and Mediterranean. They came to the Caribbean Islands and Mexico shortly after Columbus' voyages. The botanical name, Musa Sapientum, means "fruit of the wise men". This name derives from the legend that sages in India sat under banana trees during times of meditation.

It is interesting to note that the Polynesians introduced bananas throughout the Pacific region during their migrations. As a result, bananas were growing in Hawaii when the first white men arrived.

Today wise men, women, boys and girls eat bananas because they are such an excellent and nutritious food.

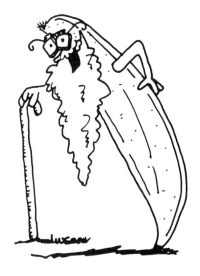

Sources of Supply

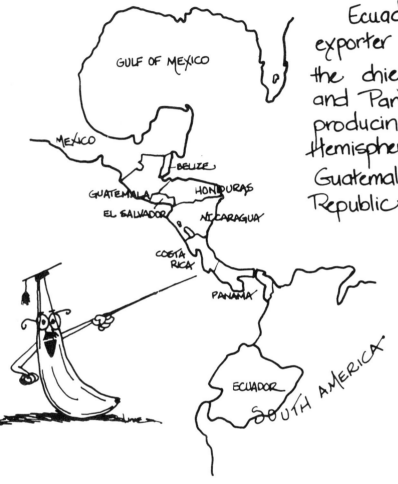

GULF OF MEXICO

MEXICO

BELIZE

GUATEMALA

HONDURAS

EL SALVADOR

NICARAGUA

COSTA RICA

PANAMA

ECUADOR

SOUTH AMERICA

Ecuador is the largest exporter of bananas. It is the chief export of Honduras and Panama. Other chief producing areas in the Western Hemisphere are Costa Rica, Guatemala, Mexico, the Dominican Republic, Brazil and Colombia.

Others in Africa are the Canary Islands, Ethiopia, Cameroon, Guinea, and Nigeria and in Asia, Taiwan.

Next time you are in a store, carefully examine the label on a bunch of bananas! Generally, the source country is named on it in small type. See how many different source countries you can find on banana labels !!

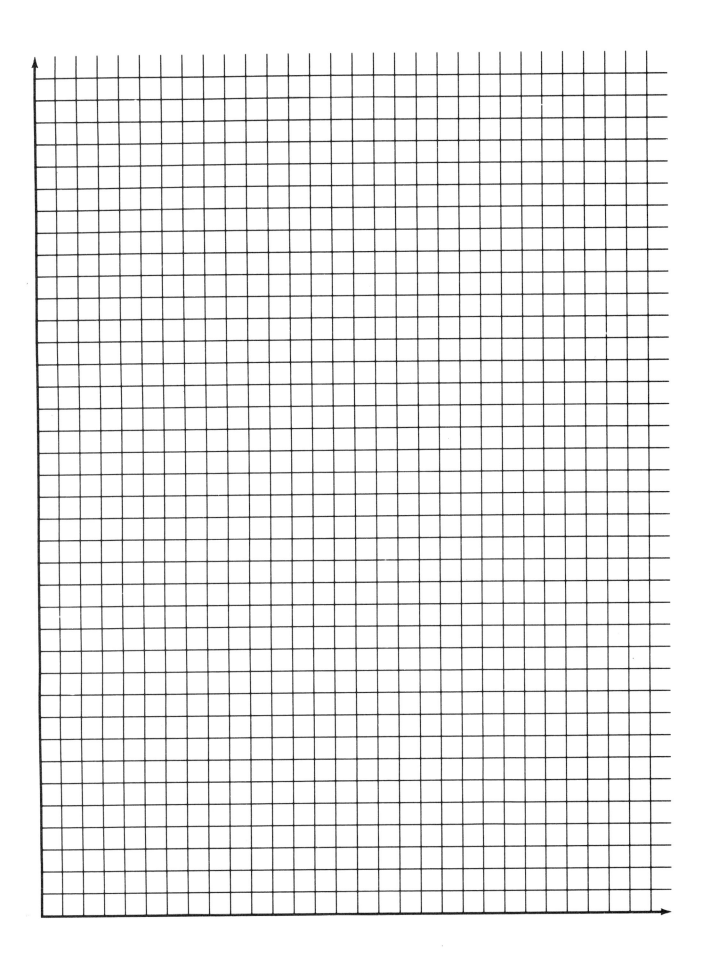

The AIMS Program

AIMS is the acronym for "**A**ctivities **I**ntegrating **M**athematics and **S**cience." Such integration enriches learning and makes it meaningful and holistic. AIMS began as a project of Fresno Pacific University to integrate the study of mathematics and science in grades K-9, but has since expanded to include language arts, social studies, and other disciplines.

AIMS is a continuing program of the non-profit AIMS Education Foundation. It had its inception in a National Science Foundation funded program whose purpose was to explore the effectiveness of integrating mathematics and science. The project directors in cooperation with 80 elementary classroom teachers devoted two years to a thorough field-testing of the results and implications of integration.

The approach met with such positive results that the decision was made to launch a program to create instructional materials incorporating this concept. Despite the fact that thoughtful educators have long recommended an integrative approach, very little appropriate material was available in 1981 when the project began. A series of writing projects have ensued and today the AIMS Education Foundation is committed to continue the creation of new integrated activities on a permanent basis.

The AIMS program is funded through the sale of this developing series of books and proceeds from the Foundation's endowment. All net income from program and products flows into a trust fund administered by the AIMS Education Foundation. Use of these funds is restricted to support of research, development, and publication of new materials. Writers donate all their rights to the Foundation to support its on-going program. No royalties are paid to the writers.

The rationale for integration lies in the fact that science, mathematics, language arts, social studies, etc., are integrally interwoven in the real world from which it follows that they should be similarly treated in the classroom where we are preparing students to live in that world. Teachers who use the AIMS program give enthusiastic endorsement to the effectiveness of this approach.

Science encompasses the art of questioning, investigating, hypothesizing, discovering, and communicating. Mathematics is a language that provides clarity, objectivity, and understanding. The language arts provide us powerful tools of communication. Many of the major contemporary societal issues stem from advancements in science and must be studied in the context of the social sciences. Therefore, it is timely that all of us take seriously a more holistic mode of educating our students. This goal motivates all who are associated with the AIMS Program. We invite you to join us in this effort.

Meaningful integration of knowledge is a major recommendation coming from the nation's professional science and mathematics associations. The American Association for the Advancement of Science in *Science for All Americans* strongly recommends the integration of mathematics, science, and technology. The National Council of Teachers of Mathematics places strong emphasis on applications of mathematics such as are found in science investigations. AIMS is fully aligned with these recommendations.

Extensive field testing of AIMS investigations confirms these beneficial results.
1. Mathematics becomes more meaningful, hence more useful, when it is applied to situations that interest students.
2. The extent to which science is studied and understood is increased, with a significant economy of time, when mathematics and science are integrated.
3. There is improved quality of learning and retention, supporting the thesis that learning which is meaningful and relevant is more effective.
4. Motivation and involvement are increased dramatically as students investigate real-world situations and participate actively in the process. We invite you to become part of this classroom teacher movement by using an integrated approach to learning and sharing any suggestions you may have. The AIMS Program welcomes you!

AIMS Education Foundation Programs

A Day with AIMS®

Intensive one-day workshops are offered to introduce educators to the philosophy and rationale of AIMS. Participants will discuss the methodology of AIMS and the strategies by which AIMS principles may be incorporated into curriculum. Each participant will take part in a variety of hands-on AIMS investigations to gain an understanding of such aspects as the scientific/mathematical content, classroom management, and connections with other curricular areas. *A Day with AIMS®* workshops may be offered anywhere in the United States. Necessary supplies and take-home materials are usually included in the enrollment fee.

A Week with AIMS®

Throughout the nation, AIMS offers many one-week workshops each year, usually in the summer. Each workshop lasts five days and includes at least 30 hours of AIMS hands-on instruction. Participants are grouped according to the grade level(s) in which they are interested. Instructors are members of the AIMS Instructional Leadership Network. Supplies for the activities and a generous supply of take-home materials are included in the enrollment fee. Sites are selected on the basis of applications submitted by educational organizations. If chosen to host a workshop, the host agency agrees to provide specified facilities and cooperate in the promotion of the workshop. The AIMS Education Foundation supplies workshop materials as well as the travel, housing, and meals for instructors.

AIMS One-Week Perspectives Workshops

Each summer, Fresno Pacific University offers AIMS one-week workshops on its campus in Fresno, California. AIMS Program Directors and highly qualified members of the AIMS National Leadership Network serve as instructors.

The AIMS Instructional Leadership Program

This is an AIMS staff-development program seeking to prepare facilitators for leadership roles in science/math education in their home districts or regions. Upon successful completion of the program, trained facilitators may become members of the AIMS Instructional Leadership Network, qualified to conduct AIMS workshops, teach AIMS in-service courses for college credit, and serve as AIMS consultants. Intensive training is provided in mathematics, science, process and thinking skills, workshop management, and other relevant topics.

College Credit and Grants

Those who participate in workshops may often qualify for college credit. If the workshop takes place on the campus of Fresno Pacific University, that institution may grant appropriate credit. If the workshop takes place off-campus, arrangements can sometimes be made for credit to be granted by another institution. In addition, the applicant's home school district is often willing to grant in-service or professional-development credit. Many educators who participate in AIMS workshops are recipients of various types of educational grants, either local or national. Nationally known foundations and funding agencies have long recognized the value of AIMS mathematics and science workshops to educators. The AIMS Education Foundation encourages educators interested in attending or hosting workshops to explore the pos- sibilities suggested above. Although the Foundation strongly supports such interest, it reminds applicants that they have the primary responsibility for fulfilling *current* requirements.

For current information regarding the programs described above, please complete the following:

Information Request

Please send current information on the items checked:

_____ *Basic Information Packet* on AIMS materials
_____ *AIMS Instructional Leadership Program*
_____ *AIMS One-Week Perspectives* workshops

_____ *A Week with AIMS®* workshops
_____ Hosting information for *A Day with AIMS®* workshops
_____ Hosting information for *A Week with AIMS®* workshops

Name _____ Phone _____

Address _____
　　　　　Street　　　　　　　　　　　　　　　　City　　　　　　　　　　　　　　State　　Zip

We invite you to subscribe to *AIMS*®!

Each issue of *AIMS*® contains a variety of material useful to educators at all grade levels. Feature articles of lasting value deal with topics such as mathematical or science concepts, curriculum, assessment, the teaching of process skills, and historical background. Several of the latest AIMS math/science investigations are always included, along with their reproducible activity sheets. As needs direct and space allows, various issues contain news of current developments, such as workshop schedules, activities of the AIMS Instructional Leadership Network, and announcements of upcoming publications.

AIMS® is published monthly, August through May. Subscriptions are on an annual basis only. A subscription entered at any time will begin with the next issue, but will also include the previous issues of that volume. Readers have preferred this arrangement because articles and activities within an annual volume are often interrelated.

Please note that an *AIMS*® subscription automatically includes duplication rights for one school site for all issues included in the subscription. Many schools build cost-effective library resources with their subscriptions.

YES! I am interested in subscribing to *AIMS*®.

Name _____   Home Phone _____

Address _____   City, State, Zip _____

Please send the following volumes (subject to availability):

_____Volume VII (1992-93) $15.00	_____Volume XII (1997-98) $30.00	
_____Volume VIII (1993-94) $15.00	_____Volume XIII (1998-99) $30.00	
_____Volume IX (1994-95) $15.00	_____Volume XIV (1999-00) $30.00	
_____Volume X (1995-96) $15.00	_____Volume XV (2000-01) $30.00	
_____Volume XI (1996-97) $30.00	_____Volume XVI (2001-02) $30.00	

_____Limited offer: Volumes XVI & XVII (2001-2003) $55.00
(Note: Prices may change without notice)

Check your method of payment:

☐ Check enclosed in the amount of $_____

☐ Purchase order attached (Please include the P.O.#, the authorizing signature, and position of the authorizing person.)

☐ Credit Card   ☐ Visa   ☐ MasterCard   Amount $ _____

Card # _____   Expiration Date _____

Signature_____   Today's Date _____

Make checks payable to **AIMS Education Foundation.**
Mail to *AIMS*® Magazine, P.O. Box 8120, Fresno, CA 93747-8120.
Phone (559) 255-4094 or (888) 733-2467   FAX (559) 255-6396
AIMS Homepage: http://www.AIMSedu.org/

AIMS Program Publications

Actions with Fractions 4-9
Bats Incredible! 2-4
Brick Layers 4-9
Brick Layers II 4-9
Cycles of Knowing and Growing 1-3
Crazy about Cotton Book 3-7
Critters K-6
Down to Earth 5-9
Electrical Connections 4-9
Exploring Environments Book K-6
Fabulous Fractions 3-6
Fall into Math and Science K-1
Field Detectives 3-6
Finding Your Bearings 4-9
Floaters and Sinkers 5-9
From Head to Toe 5-9
Fun with Foods 5-9
Glide into Winter with Math & Science K-1
Gravity Rules! Activity Book 5-12
Hardhatting in a Geo-World 3-5
It's About Time K-2
Jaw Breakers and Heart Thumpers 3-5
Just for the Fun of It! 4-9
Looking at Lines 6-9
Machine Shop 5-9
Magnificent Microworld Adventures 5-9
Math + Science, A Solution 5-9
Mostly Magnets 2-8
Multiplication the Algebra Way 4-8
Off The Wall Science 3-9
Our Wonderful World 5-9
Out of This World 4-8
Overhead and Underfoot 3-5
Paper Square Geometry:
    The Mathematics of Origami
Puzzle Play: 4-8
Pieces and Patterns 5-9
Popping With Power 3-5
Primarily Bears K-6
Primarily Earth K-3

Primarily Physics K-3
Primarily Plants K-3
Proportional Reasoning 6-9
Ray's Reflections 4-8
Sense-Able Science K-1
Soap Films and Bubbles 4-9
Spatial Visualization 4-9
Spills and Ripples 5-12
Spring into Math and Science K-1
The Amazing Circle 4-9
The Budding Botanist 3-6
The Sky's the Limit 5-9
Through the Eyes of the Explorers 5-9
Under Construction K-2
Water Precious Water 2-6
Weather Sense:
    Temperature, Air Pressure, and Wind 4-5
Winter Wonders K-2

Spanish/English Editions
Brinca de alegria hacia la Primavera con las
    Matemáticas y Ciencias K-1
Cáete de gusto hacia el Otoño con las
    Matemáticas y Ciencias K-1
Conexiones Eléctricas 4-9
El Botanista Principiante 3-6
Los Cinco Sentidos K-1
Ositos Nada Más K-6
Patine al Invierno con Matemáticas y Ciencias K-1
Piezas y Diseños 5-9
Primariamente Física K-3
Primariamente Plantas K-3
Principalmente Imanes 2-8

All Spanish/English Editions include student pages in
Spanish and teacher and student pages in English.

Spanish Edition
Constructores II: Ingeniería Creativa Con Construcciones LEGO® (4-9)
The entire book is written in Spanish. English pages not included.

Other Science and Math Publications
Historical Connections in Mathematics, Vol. I 5-9
Historical Connections in Mathematics, Vol. II 5-9
Historical Connections in Mathematics, Vol. III 5-9
Mathematicians are People, Too
Mathematicians are People, Too, Vol. II
Teaching Science with Everyday Things
What's Next, Volume 1, 4-12
What's Next, Volume 2, 4-12
What's Next, Volume 3, 4-12

For further information write to:
AIMS Education Foundation • P.O. Box 8120 • Fresno, California 93747-8120
www.AIMSedu.org/ • Fax 559•255•6396

AIMS Duplication Rights Program

AIMS has received many requests from school districts for the purchase of unlimited duplication rights to AIMS materials. In response, the AIMS Education Foundation has formulated the program outlined below. There is a built-in flexibility which, we trust, will provide for those who use AIMS materials extensively to purchase such rights for either individual activities or entire books.

It is the goal of the AIMS Education Foundation to make its materials and programs available at reasonable cost. All income from the sale of publications and duplication rights is used to support AIMS programs; hence, strict adherence to regulations governing duplication is essential. Duplication of AIMS materials beyond limits set by copyright laws and those specified below is strictly forbidden.

Limited Duplication Rights

Any purchaser of an AIMS book may make up to *200 copies* of any activity in that book for use at *one school site*. Beyond that, rights must be purchased according to the appropriate category.

Unlimited Duplication Rights for Single Activities

An individual or school may purchase the right to make an unlimited number of copies of a single activity. The royalty is $5.00 per activity per school site.

Examples: 3 activities x 1 site x $5.00 = $15.00
9 activities x 3 sites x $5.00 = $135.00

Unlimited Duplication Rights for Entire Books

A school or district may purchase the right to make an unlimited number of copies of a single, *specified* book. The royalty is $20.00 per book per school site. This is in addition to the cost of the book.

Examples: 5 books x 1 site x $20.00 = $100.00
12 books x 10 sites x $20.00 = $2400.00

Magazine/Newsletter Duplication Rights

Those who purchase *AIMS*® (magazine)/*Newsletter* are hereby granted permission to make up to 200 copies of any portion of it, provided these copies will be used for educational purposes.

Workshop Instructors' Duplication Rights

Workshop instructors may distribute to registered workshop participants a maximum of 100 copies of any article and/or 100 copies of no more than eight activities, provided these six conditions are met:

1. Since all AIMS activities are based upon the *AIMS Model of Mathematics* and the *AIMS Model of Learning*, leaders must include in their presentations an explanation of these two models.
2. Workshop instructors must relate the AIMS activities presented to these basic explanations of the AIMS philosophy of education.
3. The copyright notice must appear on all materials distributed.
4. Instructors must provide information enabling participants to order books and magazines from the Foundation.
5. Instructors must inform participants of their limited duplication rights as outlined below.
6. Only student pages may be duplicated.

Written permission must be obtained for duplication beyond the limits listed above. Additional royalty payments may be required.

Workshop Participants' Rights

Those enrolled in workshops in which AIMS student activity sheets are distributed may duplicate a maximum of 35 copies or enough to use the lessons one time with one class, whichever is less. Beyond that, rights must be purchased according to the appropriate category.

Application for Duplication Rights

The purchasing agency or individual must clearly specify the following:
1. Name, address, and telephone number
2. Titles of the books for Unlimited Duplication Rights contracts
3. Titles of activities for Unlimited Duplication Rights contracts
4. Names and addresses of school sites for which duplication rights are being purchased.

NOTE: Books to be duplicated must be purchased separately and are not included in the contract for Unlimited Duplication Rights.

The requested duplication rights are automatically authorized when proper payment is received, although a *Certificate of Duplication Rights* will be issued when the application is processed.

Address all correspondence to: **Contract Division**
AIMS Education Foundation
P.O. Box 8120
Fresno, CA 93747-8120

www.AIMSedu.org/
Fax 559•255•6396